ROUTLEDGE LIBRARY EDITIONS
BROADCASTING

Volume 8

BROADCAST SOUND
TECHNOLOGY

BROADCAST SOUND TECHNOLOGY

Second Edition

MICHAEL TALBOT-SMITH

Routledge
Taylor & Francis Group

LONDON AND NEW YORK

First published in 1995 by Focal Press

This edition first published in 2024
by Routledge
4 Park Square, Milton Park, Abingdon, Oxon OX14 4RN

and by Routledge
605 Third Avenue, New York, NY 10158

Routledge is an imprint of the Taylor & Francis Group, an informa business

British Library Cataloguing in Publication Data
A catalogue record for this book is available from the British Library

ISBN: 978-1-032-59391-3 (Set)
ISBN: 978-1-032-60780-1 (Volume 8) (hbk)
ISBN: 978-1-032-60781-8 (Volume 8) (pbk)
ISBN: 978-1-003-46051-0 (Volume 8) (ebk)

DOI: 10.4324/9781003460510

Publisher's Note
The publisher has gone to great lengths to ensure the quality of this reprint but points out that some imperfections in the original copies may be apparent.

Disclaimer
The publisher has made every effort to trace copyright holders and would welcome correspondence from those they have been unable to trace.

Broadcast Sound Technology

Second edition

Michael Talbot-Smith BSc(Hons)(Physics), CPhys, MInstP

Focal Press
An imprint of Butterworth-Heinemann Ltd
Linacre House, Jordan Hill, Oxford OX2 8DP

 A member of the Reed Elsevier plc group

OXFORD LONDON BOSTON
MUNICH NEW DELHI SINGAPORE SYDNEY
TOKYO TORONTO WELLINGTON

First published 1990
First published as a paperback edition 1992
Second edition 1995

© Butterworth-Heinemann 1995

British Library Cataloguing in Publication Data
A catalogue record for this book is available from
the British Library

ISBN 0 240 51436 X

Library of Congress Cataloguing in Publication Data
A catalogue record for this book is available from
the Library of Congress

Printed and bound in Great Britain by
Hartnolls Limited, Bodmin, Cornwall

Contents

Foreword

In this work, Michael Talbot-Smith reaps the harvest of a lifetime's teaching of sound technology for broadcasters. Working, as he did, for a renowned broadcast training establishment, Michael was a natural and dedicated instructor of young minds entering the world of radio and television audio. Together with his colleagues, he made a speciality of equipping all such students with the fundamental theoretical framework upon which to build a successful career in broadcast sound.

The seeds of knowledge were, it must be admitted, sometimes sown in reluctant minds. Infinite patience, persistence and a penetrating, friendly wit (not to mention the inevitable 'handout' of summarized information) soon lodged the necessary knowledge firmly in place. There it rested to await the inevitable day, sometimes years later, when it was still to be found as an aid to rescue a difficult programme situation. Having been subjected to Michael's techniques in this way, as were many hundreds of others, we know it works!

Now that Michael has found time to write this, the biggest 'handout' of all, the reference information necessary for broadcast sound staff is at last available to everyone. I am sure that it will prove indispensable.

Jeff Baker
BBC Television

Preface

The intention of this book is to give a clear and reasonably easy-to-read explanation of the underlying principles of modern audio technology. In trying to do this I'm aware that it is very open to criticism. Some people will feel that too many topics have been omitted. Others may think too many topics have been included, or those that are dealt with are not gone into in sufficient depth – or too deeply. It's all a matter of balance. What I have tried to do is to cover the professional audio field, from the microphones in the studio (and its acoustics) to the listener's ears, and to do this in such a way that further study will be made much easier. Inevitably there is a great deal of simplification but after some 30 years helping to train BBC technical staff I'm convinced that one of the greatest mistakes in training is to start by going into a lot of detail in already complicated subjects.

To illustrate what I mean, let's take sound desks. The majority of sound mixing desks have the same basic 'skeleton', whether they are big 50- to 60-channel consoles or whether they are portable units with six to ten channels. If the basic structure is clear then it's usually not too difficult to find the extra details of the large console reasonably easy to understand.

To put it another way, I would feel that the book had succeeded if after reading it a person could be taken into a radio or television studio for the first time and after looking round and studying the labels on the equipment, would begin to have a fair grasp of what was there, why it was there and how it functioned.

M.T.-S.

Acknowledgements

My thanks are due to the following companies, not only for giving me permission to reproduce photographs, but also supplying me with the photographs. AKG Acoustics, Ltd (photograph of C414 microphone), Audio Engineering Ltd (photograph of Micron radio microphone), AMS Industries plc (photograph of Audiofile screen display), Paul Brooke, MD, Sonifex Ltd (photograph of cartridge machine), Klark Technik plc (photograph of graphic equalizer), Messrs CEL Instruments (photograph of sound level meter), SIFAM Ltd (photographs of PPM and VU meters), Sony Broadcast and Communications (photograph of DAT recorder).

I am grateful to Paul Eaton, of BBC Transmission, who most helpfully corrected some of my mistakes about NICAM 728, and Dr A. J. Jones, of the Acoustical Investigation and Research Organization, for up-to-date information about Assisted Resonance.

I am particularly pleased to thank for their encouragement Chris Daubney, Chief Engineer of Channel 4 Television, Jeff Baker, then Head of Sound, BBC Television, Dr David Wilson of Pershore and James Gaussen, Commissioning Editor for Butterworth Scientific Ltd, for his unfailing helpfulness.

Note about the second edition

Fortunately there were very few significant errors in the first edition of this book but I am sincerely grateful to those who drew my attention to them.

I am also pleased to acknowledge the useful suggestions that I received from Keith Spencer Allen about bringing the book more up-to-date.

M.T.-S.

1 Basic sound

What are sound waves?

Strictly, we should start by defining sound waves. They are variations in air pressure capable of creating in the human ear the sensation we call 'sound'. Not all air pressure variations can cause this sensation, as we shall see later.

This chapter is the first of two about waves and their behaviour, an understanding of which is vital if later chapters are going to be really meaningful.

All types of wave have certain features in common. They all have a *frequency* – the number of complete waves passing a point in each second. They have a *velocity* – the speed at which they travel, and they have an *amplitude* – the 'height' of the wave. Broadly, there are two types of wave in nature. These are called *transverse* and *longitudinal*. It will help if we look at these separately.

Transverse waves

In a transverse wave the particles of the medium through which the wave is travelling oscillate at right angles to the direction of the wave. For example, waves in water are transverse; the medium is the water itself, and the particles are, ultimately, the water molecules. Figure 1.1 shows a transverse wave.

Interestingly, electromagnetic waves – light, radio, infra-red and X-rays, for example – are also regarded as being transverse in nature, but since they can travel through a vacuum it is not clear what, in this case, the particles are. But perhaps they are transverse in only one or two aspects.

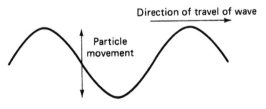

Figure 1.1 Transverse wave

Longitudinal waves

Sound waves are longitudinal, and this means that the particles of the medium – normally air, of course – oscillate in the same direction as the wave, as shown in Figure 1.2. This also shows that the air particles (in reality molecules of oxygen, nitrogen and the other constituents of the atmosphere) are displaced from what are often called their 'rest positions' – not that the air molecules are ever at rest! So there are regions of pressure which are higher than normal (*compressions*) alternating with regions of slightly lower than normal pressure (*rarefactions*). It is important to realize that these compressions and rarefactions are variations in the atmospheric pressure.

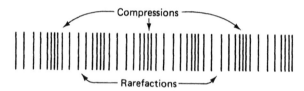

Figure 1.2 Longitudinal wave

The pressure variations are very small indeed. They correspond to the sort of pressure change that occurs with a change in altitude of the order of a few millimetres or less, which is another way of saying that the ear is an incredibly sensitive device. We shall deal with that topic in more detail later.

Figure 1.2 demonstrates what we might see if sound waves could somehow be made visible, but such a diagram is inconvenient to represent. It doesn't show at all clearly the size, or amplitude, of the wave. It is much easier to deal with *pressure graphs*, as in Figure 1.3. This is easier to draw and more meaningful, as with this type of representation it is possible to show variations in the shape of the wave. There are other characteristics of sound waves which can be plotted – the *particle displacement*, for example – but pressure is the most useful because after all it is the pressure changes in the air which affect our eardrums and the diaphragms of microphones.

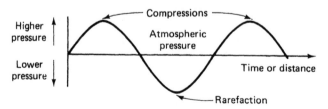

Figure 1.3 A pressure graph

The velocity of sound waves

The speed at which sound waves travel depends on the medium through which they are travelling. Table 1.1 gives the velocity of sound in various well-known substances. It may be debatable, following the definition at the start of this chapter, whether we can call longitudinal waves in, say wood, sound waves, since we can only hear them when they pass from the air into our ears, but perhaps this is splitting hairs!

Table 1.1 Velocities of sound

Substance	Velocity of sound (metres/second)
Fresh water	1480
Glass	5200
Concrete	3400
Steel	5000–5900
Wood	3000–4000
Carbon dioxide	[a]259
Oxygen	[a]316
Hydrogen	[a]1284
Helium	[a]965
Air	340

[a] For these gases the velocity is that at 0°C
The fact that the velocity of sound in helium is some two and a half times that in air accounts for the high-pitched voices of divers and others who breath an oxygen-helium mixture.

The velocity of sound in air

The velocity of sound waves in any gas is given by

$$c = \sqrt{\frac{\gamma P}{p}}$$

where c is the velocity, γ is the ratio of the specific heats of the gas (for air this can be taken as 1.414), P is the gas pressure and p is the gas density.

Although the density of the gas (p) appears in the equation, in practice, with sound waves in the atmosphere, if the barometric pressure rises then the air density increases also, in the same proportion. This follows from the well-known Boyle's Law. Consequently the velocity of sound does not vary with changes in atmospheric pressure – at least over all reasonable ranges of conditions. The velocity of sound *does* go down at high altitudes, and it is widely thought that this is because of the lower air pressure. In fact this is not the true explanation. Lower temperatures are the cause, as we can easily see.

At a constant pressure the volume of a gas, other things being equal, varies as its absolute temperature. This is measured in kelvins, so that $0\,K = -273°C$. Or $0°C = 273\,K$.

Thus, for every °C rise in temperature the volume of the gas increases by 1/273 of its original volume. This means that the density *decreases* in the same proportion. From the equation above, if the density decreases, the velocity goes up. (We're assuming the gas obeys Boyle's Law. For air at all normal pressure and temperature ranges this is a valid assumption.) In other words:

higher temperature . . . higher velocity
lower temperature . . . lower velocity

For air, then, a calculation to find the velocity at a temperature t is:

c (m/s) $= 331 + 0.6\,t$

This gives the velocity of sound as:

325 m/s at $-10°C$
331 m/s at $0°C$
337 m/s at $+10°C$
343 m/s at $+20°C$

For almost all practical purposes we can take c at room temperatures as 340 m/s.

In alternative units, c is about 760 miles/hour, 1100 feet/second, and 1 mile in roughly 5 seconds. It may be worth comparing these figures with the velocity of electromagnetic waves, which is 300 000 km/s (186 000 miles/s) in free space and only very slightly less in air.

Wavelength

This is often a convenient term. Wavelength, usually denoted by the Greek letter λ (lambda), is the distance between corresponding points on adjacent cycles. See Figure 1.4.

There is a very important relationship between frequency, velocity and wavelength:

$c = f\lambda$

f being the frequency. This applies to any wave – it's just as true for radio waves as it is for sound waves. It doesn't always work too well for water

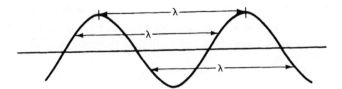

Figure 1.4 Wavelength

waves because in their case the velocity is apt to vary with the amplitude of the wave, but that need not worry us here. For sound waves at room temperature Table 1.2 gives the approximate wavelength for different frequencies. The frequency range is from 16 Hz to 16 kHz, which is roughly the hearing range for a normal adult. (This point will be gone into later, in Chapter 3.) There are two points to notice.

Table 1.2 Wavelengths for different frequencies

Frequency	Wavelength	
16 Hz	21.25 m	69 ft
20 Hz	17 m	55 ft
50 Hz	6.8 m	22 ft
100 Hz	3.4 m	11 ft
500 Hz	68 cm	2.2 ft
1 kHz	34 cm	1.1 ft
2 kHz	17 cm	6.6 in
5 kHz	6.8 cm	2.7 in
10 kHz	3.4 cm	1.4 in
16 kHz	2.1 cm	0.8 in

First, it is very easy to calculate *roughly* the wavelength for any given frequency, or vice versa. It is only necessary to remember that at a frequency of 1 kHz the wavelength is about ⅓ metre or 1 foot. Then it is simply a matter of proportion. For example, to find the wavelength of a sound of frequency 200 Hz: this is one-fifth of 1 kHz so the wavelength will be five times greater; that is 5 × ⅓ m = 1⅔ m, or 5 × 1 ft = 5 ft. This sort of accuracy is quite good enough for the great majority of sound calculations.

The second point to note is the great range of sound wave frequencies: about 1000:1 in fact. Compare this with light where the longest waves (red) have a wavelength of around 700 nm (nanometres) and the shortest (blue-violet) have a wavelength of 400 nm – a ratio of less than 2:1. As we shall see, the behaviour of waves depends very much on their wavelength, so a frequent difficulty in sound work is that the waves vary greatly in their properties at different parts of the frequency range.

In Chapter 2 one of the things we will be dealing with is *why* the great range of sound wavelengths causes difficulties.

2 The behaviour of sound waves

Reflection and diffraction

Everyone is familiar with the echo which results from a loud noise being reflected back from the side of a large building or a cliff. This may lead one to imagine that sound waves are always reflected back from rigid obstacles. In fact they may *not* be. Whether waves (and this is true for all waves) are reflected from an obstacle or not depends on the relationship between their wavelength and the size of the obstacle. Perhaps surprisingly, the dimension of the obstacle which is important in this context is that at *right-angles* to the direction of the wave. Broadly speaking, if the wavelength is *less* than the size of the obstacle then reflection occurs. If the wavelength is *greater* than the size of the obstacle then reflection does not occur and *diffraction* takes place. Diffraction will be explained more fully in a moment. Figure 2.1 shows the conditions for reflection to take place.

The statement above, that reflection occurs if wavelength is less than obstacle size, is only roughly correct. Figure 2.2 shows more accurately the relationship between wavelength/obstacle size and amount of reflection. This is a somewhat idealized curve. In practice there will be irregularities which will depend on the exact shape of the obstacle. It is, however, approximately correct to say that there is about 100% reflection if the obstacle's size (i.e. its dimension at right angles to the direction of the wave) is three or more times greater than the wavelength, there is virtually no reflection if the obstacle is one-third of the wavelength, and when the wavelength equals the obstacle size there is about 50% reflection.

We can now see why the enormous frequency (or wavelength) range of sound waves can present problems. Imagine, for example, a studio in which sound recordings are made. In all probability there will be music stands, perhaps equivalent to half a metre, as obstacles; there will be musical instruments of a variety of sizes; there could be an assortment of screens. All these differently sized objects will have their own reflection characteristics; the smaller items will reflect only the higher frequencies, the very large ones will reflect all but the low frequencies, and so on.

Diffraction is, in a sense, a complementary effect to reflection. It is said to occur when waves *bend round* an obstacle. Thus, when relatively long wavelengths meet an obstacle we know that there will be little or no reflection.

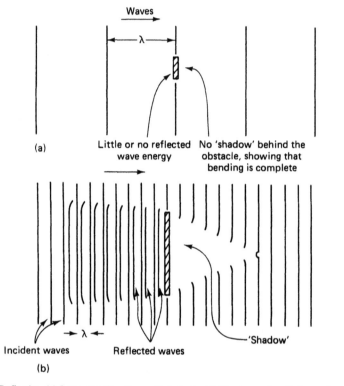

Figure 2.1 Reflection (a) Long wavelength, small obstacle; (b) Short wavelength, large obstacle

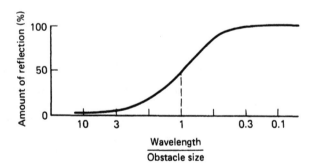

Figure 2.2 Percentage reflection for different values of wavelength/obstacle size

Instead the waves bend round the obstacle and diffraction occurs. In other words, if there is marked reflection there is little diffraction; if there is little reflection then there must be considerable diffraction taking place.

Some very interesting and important effects occur when waves pass through an *aperture*. As Figure 2.3 shows, if the aperture is much larger than wavelength the emerging waves tend to form a more or less parallel-sided beam. If the wavelength is small then a marked spreading occurs.

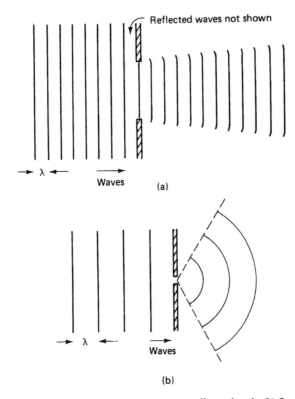

Figure 2.3 Diffraction at an aperture (a) Large aperture, small wavelength; (b) Small aperture, large wavelength

Later we shall see that this is important in understanding the behaviour of loudspeakers, because a loudspeaker is basically one or more holes (apertures) in a cabinet and waves are generated on one side of these holes.

It is interesting to note that both reflection and diffraction effects take place with *all* types of wave. They can often be seen particularly well in the case of water with waves entering a small harbour. It is surprising how one can improve one's understanding of waves by standing, apparently idly, on jetties!

The effects of reflection of light are so obvious that we take them for granted, but this is only because everyday objects are so much bigger than light wavelengths that reflection is virtually 100%. Diffraction *does* happen with light but it usually has to be carefully looked for.

The inverse square law

There is one other important topic to deal with at this stage. It is the way in which waves radiate when there are no obstructions. For simplicity we will imagine that they originate in what is called a *point source* – theoretically an infinitely small source. In practice, of course, such things do not exist but there are good approximations to them when the source is small compared with wavelength. The waves in such a case will take the form of concentric spheres, with the source at their centre. It is fairly obvious that the wave energy will weaken the further away they get from their origin. In fact the *intensity*, which at the moment we will simply call the energy in the wave, diminishes in inverse proportion to the *square* of the distance from the source:

$$I \propto \frac{1}{d^2}$$

where I is the intensity and d is the distance from the source – *the inverse square law*. Put another way, doubling the distance from the source causes the intensity to decrease to one-quarter, and so on.

We have avoided defining intensity so far. In fact it is nothing more than the power passing through a unit area, and the normal unit is watts per square metre (W/m^2). To give some meaning to this unit it may be helpful to point out that, at its most sensitive, the average human ear can respond to a sound intensity of about $10^{-12}\,W/m^2$; speech heard from a distance of 1 m will have an intensity at the listener's ear of around $10^{-6}\,W/m^2$ ($1\,\mu W/m^2$); and very loud sounds have an intensity of perhaps $1\,mW/m^2$. And if we do out best to visualize only $1\,mW$ of power spread out over a full square metre, there isn't a great deal of energy going into the ear! In fact, the figure of $10^{-12}\,W/m^2$, the intensity needed to make the ear respond at its most sensitive, is comparable to the light power from a small torch bulb at a distance of the order of 100 km.

Before we leave the subject of the inverse square law there are two terms we should mention – *plane waves* and *spherical waves*. We have already seen that if there is a small source the waves radiating from it will be in the form of concentric spheres. They will be *spherical waves*. However, this curvature will only be noticeable at relatively short distances away from the source – in what is sometimes called the *near field*. At a considerable distance the curvature will not be very obvious, at least not to an observer in the midst of the waves. They are then called *plane waves*. The distinction between plane and spherical waves is never very clear; after all, there will be *some* curvature at whatever distance from the source. Unfortunately, considerable importance is sometimes given to whether waves are plane or spherical – usually quite unnecessarily. In this book we shall try to avoid such confusion by simply saying whether we are thinking about conditions close to or a long way from a source of waves.

Decibels

Having just introduced intensity in W/m^2, or more realistically $\mu W/m^2$, we are going to move on to a much more convenient unit, but unfortunately one which almost always causes confusion in people's minds when they first come across it – the *decibel* (dB).

Essentially the decibel is a unit of *change in power* or, in electrical contexts, a change in either power or voltage. If, for whatever reason, there is a doubling of the power we can say that there has been an increase of 3 dB. Imagine an electrical signal being amplified by a suitable item of electronic apparatus. Whatever signal power is at the input, if the output power is twice as much then we can say the *gain* of the amplifier is 3 dB. If there is *four* times as much power then the gain is $3 + 3 = 6$ dB.

The mathematics of this is based on the definition of the decibel as being:

$$\text{dB change} = 10 \log_{10} (\text{power ratio})$$

If the power ratio is $2:1$, then

$$\text{dB change} = 10 \log 2$$
$$= 10 \times 0.301$$
$$= 3.01 \text{ dB (in practice 3 dB is usually near enough)}$$

If the power ratio is $4:1$, then

$$\text{dB change} = 10 \log 4$$
$$= 10 \times 0.602$$
$$= 6 \text{ dB (approximately)}$$

And finally a power ratio of $10:1$ results in

$$\text{dB change} = 10 \log 10$$
$$= 10 \times 1$$
$$= 10 \text{ dB}$$

Table 2.1 Table of decibels for different power ratios

Power ratios	Decibels
10^6	60
10^3	30
100	20
50	17
20	13
10	10
5	7
3	4.8
2	3.0
1	0.00
0.5	−3.0

Table 2.1 sets out the decibels corresponding to a range of power ratios. The reader might find it worth his or her while to use a pocket calculator to verify these ratios.

One point to realize is that if the ratio is *less* than 1 the number of decibels is unchanged; a minus sign (−) is put in front.

Now we must relate decibels to sound as perceived by the ear. Because the definition of the decibel involves logarithms we can quite legitimately call it a *logarithmic* unit. It so happens that the ear responds to sound intensities *logarithmically*. This means that the decibel is very convenient to use in relation to hearing. It wasn't originally intended for this, having been devised as a useful unit in connection with what we would now call 'communication engineering'. However, there are three useful facts:

1. The ear can just detect a change of 1 dB in a steady tone.
2. It can just detect a change of 3 dB in speech or music.
3. A change of 10 dB represents, to most people, approximately a doubling (or halving) of the loudness.

A word of caution here: what has been said so far could imply that *loudness* and *power* or *intensity* are very closely related. *This is not so.* There is a link between loudness and power or intensity, but it is not a straightforward one. We shall look at it in Chapter 3.

Measuring sound pressure

Various units are, or have been, used in measuring sound pressure (acoustic force per unit area). The following is a selection.

- **dyne/cm²**   This is only likely to be found in older books. It was the standard unit in the centimetre-gramme-second (cgs) system. A moderately loud sound – around 60 dBA (see Chapter 3) – has a sound pressure of about 1 dyne/cm².
- **newton/metre² (N/m²)**   A newton is the force which will give a mass of 1 kg an acceleration of 1 m/s² (Sir Isaac Newton, 1642–1727, British mathematician and physicist):

$$1\,N/m^2 = 10 \text{ dyne/cm}^2$$

The name which is increasingly used for this unit is the pascal (Blaise Pascal, 1623–1662, French mathematician and physicist):

$$1\,Pa = 1\,N/m^2$$

- **bar**   One bar is approximately normal atmospheric pressure. Most weather charts give pressures in millibars (mb).

$$1 \quad bar = 10^6 \text{ dynes/cm}^2$$

$$1\,\mu\,bar = 1 \text{ dyne/cm}^2$$

$$10\,\mu\,bar = 1\,N/m^2 = 1\,Pa$$

Of less interest in acoustics, but included here for completeness, is the torr:

$$1 \text{ atmosphere} = 1.01325 \times 10^5 \text{ Pa}$$

$$1\,torr = 133.322\,Pa = 1/760 \text{ atmosphere}$$

(The torr is named after Evangelista Torricelli, 1608–1647, Italian physicist.)

3 Aspects of hearing

The ear and the hearing process

We sometimes talk about the ear as if the only part that mattered were the visible organs on either side of the head! In fact these (medical term: *pinnae*) are almost the least important parts. Far more important and complex is the structure inside the head, consisting of what are generally known as the *middle* and *inner* ears. First there is a mechanical reaction to the sound vibrations reaching the ear. Then, as we shall see, neurological signals in the form of pulses are sent to the brain. Finally, the brain interprets these signals to produce the sensation we call hearing. It is often not easy to be quite sure which of these three processes is primarily involved when we look at any aspect of hearing. All three will be outlined in this chapter. At the moment the important thing is to remember that when, for convenience, we talk about the ear, in reality we are usually, by implication, talking about the ear–brain complex.

Let us first look at the physical part of the ear and how it works, although it must be said that there are still some unanswered questions about this complicated mechanism. Figure 3.1 shows, in a very simplified form, a section through the ear.

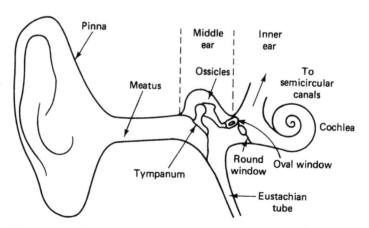

Figure 3.1 Section through the ear

The visible portion is called, as we said above, the *pinna*. Its function in humans is probably rather subtle. It isn't big enough to be able to reflect significant amounts of sound into the rest of the mechanism, unlike in some animals such as dogs, which can detect very high frequencies and consequently very short wavelengths. They can probably use their ears to help collect sound waves because some, at least, of the wavelengths are small enough to be reflected by the animal's outer ear.

There is recent evidence which suggests that in humans the pinna is of some use in locating sound directions, especially from behind, when it is thought that the ridges in it cause different patterns of reflection for the very short wavelengths, depending on whether the sounds come from the front or the rear.

The channel, the *meatus*, is about 2.5 cm long and conveys the sound waves to the eardrum (*tympanum*). This is a delicate membrane. It is slightly conical and has attached to it a muscle which tightens when very loud sounds strike the eardrum, thus reducing the risk of damage. Damage can still occur to the eardrum because of very intense noises, but in a person in good health a damaged eardrum will often heal within a few weeks. In the middle ear, to the right of the eardrum in the figure, is a chain of three small bones, the *ossicles*. They have a very important function – they act as a mechanical transformer. In the inner ear the sound vibrations travel in fluid, while until they reach the eardrum they are, of course, travelling in air. Now if sound waves meet a change in the medium in which they are travelling there is a tendency for reflection to occur – the bigger the change the more the reflection. So when sound waves meet water, or any other liquid, very little energy goes into the water. (Swimmers under water will have noticed that they do not hear much of any noises above the surface.) The job of the ossicles, then, is to *transform* the low-pressure movements of the eardrum into a higher pressure, but smaller amplitude, movement for the fluid in the inner ear. A very effective transfer of sound wave energy is carried out. The tube joining the middle ear, the *Eustachian tube*, goes down to the back of the nose and throat. It is normally closed but opens when we swallow. It can thus equalize atmospheric pressure changes on both sides of the ear drum – 'the blocked ear' sensation when one has a cold is likely to be a blocked Eustachian tube, preventing equalization of air pressures.

It is in the inner ear that conversion of sound vibrations into nerve pulses takes place. (The semi-circular canals at the top help us to keep our balance. They don't play any part in the hearing process.) The inner ear consists of a spiral cavity in the bone. It is called the *cochlea* from the Latin word meaning 'shell' and would look rather like a snail shell with about two and a half turns. It is about 3 cm long. Figure 3.2 represents the cochlea if it could be straightened out.

The sound vibrations enter the cochlea at the 'oval window' (*fenestre ovalis*) and from there on they are, as we have said, travelling in a watery fluid. Dividing the upper and lower sections of the cochlea is a membrane (the *basilar membrane*), itself a complex structure. The vibrations travel along the upper

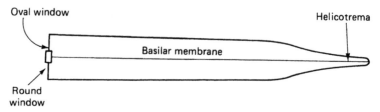

Figure 3.2 The cochlea

section of the cochlea, through a very small hole, the *helicotrema*, and back down to the *round window*. The latter exists because fluids are almost incompressible, and if the round window, which is a flexible membrane, did not exist to move outwards slightly when the oval window moves in, then very little movement of the oval window could take place.

The structure of the basilar membrane is too complex to describe briefly. It must be enough here to say that it responds to different sound frequencies at different places. It used to be thought that the basilar membrane was a set of resonators, rather like the strings of piano. This is now known not to be the case. The way in which this frequency analysis happens is much more complicated. Surprisingly, the membrane responds to the highest frequencies at its widest part (near the oval window) and to the lowest frequencies near the helicotrema. Along the length of the membrane and its associated structures there are *hair cells*, which, when stimulated by vibration, send electrical signals to the brain.

These signals are in the form of small electrical pulses. They are of constant amplitude and vary only in frequency – loud noises producing several hundred pulses each second. The way in which different frequencies are conveyed to the brain is by separate nerves – very many thousands of them – which end in the *cerebral cortex*, the outer part of the brain at the back of the head. From there onwards it is the brain's *interpretation* of these nerve pulses which is important, and that is not at all well understood! However, we shall later make reference to some of the effects of this interpretation, even if explanations are scanty.

The ear's response to different frequencies

We tend to assume that items of audio equipment respond more or less equally to all frequencies over a reasonably wide range – sometimes an erroneous assumption, but with almost always a degree of truth. The ear is different, however. Its response is far from even, except for fairly loud sounds. Figure 3.3 shows what is known as the curve for the threshold of hearing (or threshold of audibility). It shows the sound pressures needed just to produce an audible effect at different frequencies. Below the curve represents silence.

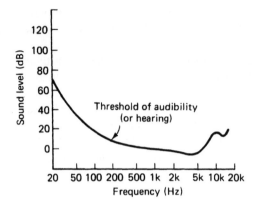

Figure 3.3 Threshold of hearing curve

First, notice the axes. The horizontal axis goes from about 16 Hz to 16 kHz, these being the approximate frequency limits of hearing for the average adult. We can sometimes *feel* as a fluttering effect in the ears frequencies below 16 Hz, but such frequencies have no musical note. Figures of 18 Hz and 20 Hz are sometimes given as the lowest frequency that can be heard. The fact is that it is very difficult actually to measure the lower limit – 16 Hz is as good a value as any!

Frequencies *above* 16 kHz can be heard by younger people. Children can often detect sounds well above 20 kHz, but by the time the average person is into his or her middle twenties 16 kHz is a fairly reasonable figure to adopt. The upper limit in particular decreases with age but there seems to be so much variation between individuals that it is unwise to try to be specific.

The vertical axis in the diagram is sound level. At the bottom of the scale the pressure, which is roughly that required to create a sound at about 3 kHz, is very small – 0.00002 N/m^2. This is close to the sound intensity of 10^{-12}W/m^2 that we met in Chapter 2.

The important thing to notice about the graph is that it is far from flat. The average ear is very sensitive indeed at about 3 kHz but is far less sensitive at 16 Hz, when the pressures have to be some *ten thousand times greater* to cause an audible sensation. It is also markedly less sensitive at the 16 kHz end of the range.

A curious characteristic of the ear is that its response curve becomes flatter at higher listening levels. Figure 3.4 illustrates this, plotting what are known as *equal loudness curves*.

The curves in Figure 3.4 are known as the *NPL curves*, from the National Physical Laboratory at Teddington, Middlesex, UK, where they were derived experimentally in the 1960s. The work was a refinement of earlier research, again experimental, by *Fletcher* and *Munsen* in the USA in the 1930s. (The curves are sometimes called the 'Fletcher–Munsen curves'.)

The important point about the equal loudness curves is that each line is just that – a plot of equally loud sensations shown for a range of frequencies.

There is an easy experiment to show the insensitivity of the ear to low frequencies at quiet listening levels. Listen, at a comfortably loud level, to almost any piece of music with a reasonable bass content. Then turn the volume down until the music is quiet. It will sound rather 'thin' and 'tinny' and will appear to be very lacking in bass. This is not caused by any defect in the volume control or the loudspeakers. It is due entirely to the fact that at low listening levels the ear's response to bass sounds is poor. Many home sound systems have a

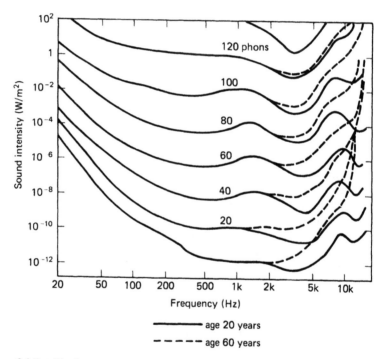

Figure 3.4 Equal loudness curves

switchable control, often labelled 'Loudness', which attempts to compensate for this by automatically increasing the bass content when the volume control is at a low setting.

Of course, the ear's response at the high frequencies also decreases but this effect is less noticeable because the higher frequencies in most music contain less energy than the low ones. (Many people will listen cheerfully to medium wave radio, when there is rarely anything above 3–4 kHz present.)

It is important to realize that the equal loudness curves in Figure 3.4 are *average* ones, based on measurements made with a large number of people.

The top curve in Figure 3.4 represents the maximum sound level which can still be called a sound. Because it also represents the onset of a different physical sensation it is known as *the threshold of pain* or *the threshold of feeling*.

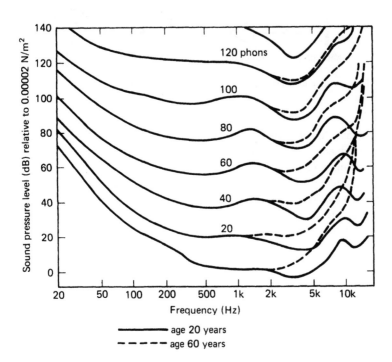

Figure 3.5 Equal loudness curves and a decibel scale

So far we have used the concept of sound *pressure* and the units have been N/m² (or pascals). In fact it is usually much more convenient to adopt decibels as units. If so, since the decibel is a unit of *comparison* we must adopt a Standard Reference for 0 dB. The universally adopted reference is a sound pressure of 0.00002 N/m², or 0.00002 Pa. This pressure is close to that needed to create a sensation of sound at 3 kHz. Figure 3.5 shows the equal loudness curves again, but this time with a vertical axis marked in decibels.

Loudness and the phon

The *phon* is a unit of loudness, but as loudness is a subjective phenomenon, and perceptions of loudness may differ from one person to another, it is perhaps not a very useful unit. The easiest way of explaining it is to say that a sound has a loudness of *n* phons when it has the same loudness as a sound of 1 kHz frequency *n* dB above the reference zero. Thus the 60 phon loudness curve is the one which passes through the 60 dB sound level at 1 kHz.

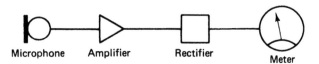

Microphone   Amplifier   Rectifier   Meter

Figure 3.6 A possible loudness indicating device for loud sounds

The measurement of loudness presents a problem. Since it is, as we have said, a purely subjective effect there is no way in which any instrument can detect what is being perceived in a person's brain. It might seem that the arrangement of microphone, amplifier and meter shown in Figure 3.6 would do this job, but a moment's thought will show that such a device will be approximately accurate only when the ear's response is fairly flat, i.e. for loud sounds. When quiet sounds are to be measured the arrangement in Figure 3.6 could give high readings for sounds of, say, 20 Hz when they might be quite inaudible!

Table 3.1 Measurements in dBA

Description	dBA	Example of noise
Painful	140	Jet engine, near
Deafening	120	Jet aircraft at 150 m
	100	Loud motor horn at 5 m
		Orchestra, fortissimo at 5 m
Very loud	95	Small jet aircraft at 150 m
	90	Busy street; workshop
	80	Average orchestra at 5 m
Loud	70	Radio set, full volume at 2 m
	60	Normal conversation at 1 m
Moderate	50	Inside fairly quiet car
	40	Inside quiet house
Faint	30	Whisper at 1 m
	20	Inside very quiet country church
Very faint	10	Sound-proofed room
Just detectable	5	Threshold of hearing

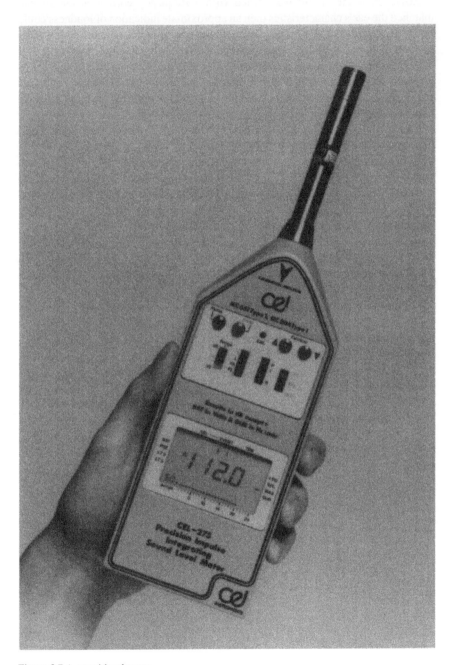

Figure 3.7 A sound level meter

However, if the circuit were fitted with a frequency correction circuit that matched the ear's characteristics then an approximate indication of loudness could be given. The idea of using a *weighting network* to do this is not new. Many years ago international agreement was reached on three such networks, known as A, B and C, to correspond to the average ear's response at low, medium and high levels respectively. Devices using these networks are now fairly common, although rarely cheap. They are sometimes called 'loudness meters', but are more properly named *sound level meters*. Figure 3.7 shows a typical instrument.

The meter is calibrated in decibels – often in a number of ranges – and measurements made should be quoted as *n* dBA, or whatever letter is appropriate. The original intention was that the network was chosen to suit the level of sound being measured. However, it has been found that the A network seems to correlate reasonably well with perceptions of loudness, no matter what the sound level is. Consequently measurements quoted as so many dBA are very widely encountered. Table 3.1 gives some typical measurements in dBA.

It should be noted that the ear is good at detecting *changes* in loudness but it is a very unreliable judge of *absolute* loudness (or levels in dBA). To begin with, the degree of *annoyance* affects one's judgement. To a rock music fan, a Mozart symphony may seem unbearably loud, when, to the Mozart lover, it is just comfortable! (Vice versa situations are perhaps more common.) Also the frequency and time of day or night of a sound contribute to a person's assessment. A single quiet aircraft at 3.0 a.m. may seem much louder than a noisier one in the middle of the afternoon.

4 Harming and charming the ear

Hearing impairment

There are broadly two consequences of excessively loud sounds. One is called *temporary threshold shift* (TTS) and is generally regarded as harmless if it doesn't occur too often. It is experienced by most people from time to time and is simply a short duration 'deafness' – in reality, loss of sensitivity – caused by, for example, a nearby gunshot. TTS may last for only a few seconds or for as much as many minutes. More serious is *permanent threshold shift* (PTS), from which there is no recovery. Actual damage is done to the delicate structures on the basilar membrane. The exact conditions for producing PTS are not known. Studies of people suffering from PTS can only be retrospective, possibly over very many years.

The present view in the UK and the rest of Europe is that there is probably little risk of hearing impairment for sound levels less than 90 dBA, although it is a requirement in the UK that in an industrial situation ear defenders are made available when the noise level reaches 85 dBA. A sound level of 90 dBA could, it is felt, be endured for 8 hours a day, 5 days a week for many years without damage, although such conditions for work would be far from pleasant. For higher level sounds the basic rule that is adopted is that for every 3 dB increase in level the exposure should be halved, as shown in Table 4.1.

There have been attempts to control the sound levels of, for example, discos, but legislation is difficult. In addition, it is not known to what extent individuals

Table 4.1 Decibel levels and exposure

dB	hours/day	days/week
90	8	5
93	4	5
96	2	5
99	1	5
102	½	5
and so on		

differ in their susceptibility – some may be more prone to hearing damage than others. A further difficulty is in measuring the sound levels. Few of the possibly hazardous levels are constant. A typical noisy environment is not likely to be equally noisy all the time. Consequently measurements with a simple sound level meter are not very informative. What is needed is a means of determining the *equivalent sound level*, L_{eq}. To explain this let us take an L_{eq} of 92 dBA. This means that whatever variations there may be in the sound level, the equivalent over a suitably long period is a steady sound of 92 dBA. There may be short periods of very high levels – perhaps 95 or even 100 dBA, but if these really are brief and the rest of the time sound levels are low, maybe conversational levels of around 60 dBA, then the L_{eq} could easily be no more than 70 dBA over a working day. On the other hand the times of high sound levels could be long enough for the L_{eq} to be over 90 dBA, in which case there is a potential hearing hazard. Measurement therefore means having a device which integrates the sound levels over as long a period as is required – possibly 8 hours in an industrial environment. Such *noise dosage meters* have in the past been very expensive, although relatively low cost instruments are now being made. (The term $L_{e,pd}$ – the equivalent level for a person on a daily basis – is used rather than L_{eq} for noise dosage.)

Pitch

The *pitch* of a musical note is usually described, somewhat vaguely, as the position of that note in the musical scale. This is a perfectly good definition if everyone knows what a musical scale is! However, we have to start somewhere, so other than offering the equally vague idea that pitch is the 'highness' or 'lowness' of a note we will assume that no further attempts at description are needed.

It is generally assumed that pitch and frequency are the same thing. This is nearly but not quite true. *Frequency* is a measurable quantity. *Pitch* is, like loudness, a purely subjective effect and cannot therefore be measured. Luckily, though, there is a good (but not perfect) correlation between pitch and frequency, and it is permissible to assume that the two are almost synonymous. Later we will show the nature of the discrepancy which can exist.

Ignoring any discrepancies, the easiest way to deal with pitch is to start with a diagram of a keyboard such as that of a piano and mark it with at least some of the frequencies allotted to the notes, as in Figure 4.1. This is a simplification. For example, on any keyboard C sharp and D flat are the same. But a person with a good musical ear finds that these notes, which can be produced as separate notes on, for example, a violin, are *not* exactly the same. The whole business of pitch is full of complications; what we set out here must of necessity avoid these problems. Some things can be outlined though.

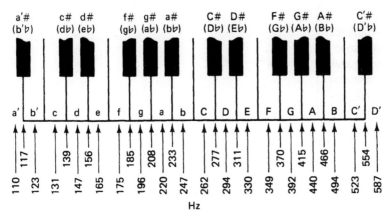

Figure 4.1 Keyboard with frequencies

Octaves

The curious fact is that notes whose frequencies are related in the sequence 1:2:4:8:16, etc. have, to the ear, something in common. They are, in a sense, all versions of the same note. A female singer hearing a note of frequency 100 Hz would be unable to sing it, so she would sing a note having a frequency of probably 400 Hz. This would be quite acceptable and sound in tune.

It is worth noting here that in going up in octaves the frequencies are following a logarithmic series. It is not only loudness that is based on a logarithmic law, pitch is also.

Why the word octave, which implies a connection with eight? This is simply because the most basic musical scale of all, the kind we are taught to sing which goes 'doh, re, me, fa, so, la, te, doh' and which 'sounds right', consists of eight notes in going from one 'doh' to the next, which is an octave higher.

We can see a logarithmic law at work if we look more closely at the keyboard in Figure 4.1. In going from any note to the one an octave above it we find that if we include the black notes, there are 12 in each octave. These are known as *semitones*. Since there are 12 to each octave, and each octave represents a doubling of frequency (or halving if we are going down), it follows that the frequency ratio of any note to the one a semitone above is $^{12}\sqrt{2}$ or $2^{1/12}$. This works out as 1.05946, or about 6%. (It is a useful exercise to take a pocket calculator, evaluate $2^{1/12}$ and then, starting with any convenient frequency, multiply repeatedly by this number to verify that after 12 operations you are at twice the starting frequency.)

It is not easy to explain why there are 12 equal increments, each of about 6%, to an octave but that a natural scale consists of eight notes. To our ears a natural-sounding scale is made up of the ascending sequence:

2 semitones
2 semitones
1 semitone
2 semitones } 8 steps
2 semitones
2 semitones
1 semitone

Total 12 semitones

Using the sequence above non-musicians can puzzle out for themselves that the scale of C (starting on C) needs no black notes; the scale of D needs two – C sharp and F sharp, and so on.

One final matter before we leave pitch; there is no fundamental law which says that any particular note *must* have a certain frequency. In other words, we could decide that middle C was to have a frequency of 250 Hz, and provided all the other notes fitted round that in the way we have outlined above we would have a perfectly valid set of musical notes. This, in the past, was rather the state of affairs. Different builders of pipe organs had their own ideas of correct pitch, and certainly up to the earlier years of this century brass bands often had their own pitch. This anarchic situation did not matter all that much until broadcasting and recording became international, when it became obviously important to have agreement between all the countries involved. In May 1939 an international conference was held in London and it was settled that A above middle C was to have a frequency of 440 Hz. (It has been suggested that this was the last international conference ever to reach agreement on anything!) This gives middle C a frequency of 261 Hz – but beware of some tuning forks still in existence, especially in school physics labs! These may be in a 'scientific' pitch, which has C = 256 Hz, so that on this system A is about 430 Hz.

Pitch and loudness

We said earlier that pitch and loudness could not be exactly related. The curious fact is that pitch is affected, albeit only slightly, by loudness. A simple experiment is to play a pure tone over a loudspeaker at moderate loudness and then to turn down the volume rapidly so that the sound is very much quieter. Almost invariably a slight change in pitch will be noticed – probably not more than a semitone. The effect seems to vary with individuals and also upon the frequency. For example, the pitch of a low frequency sound may go up and the pitch of a high frequency sound may go down; furthermore different people may experience opposite effects. There seems to be no simple explanation.

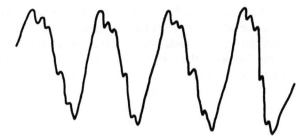

Figure 4.2 A typical 'real' sound waveform

Harmonics

In Chapter 1 we represented sound waves by a pure waveform (a *sine* wave, since it is a plot of trigonometrical sines). Sound waves in real life have a very different appearance if examined with, say, a microphone and oscilloscope. Figure 4.2 is typical. We must state three things about the kind of waveform shown in Figure 4.2:

1. The waveform is *repetitive*, that is, each complete cycle is exactly like the one before it and the one after it.
2. In real life, and this seems to negate what we have just said, a study on a suitable screen will almost always show some slight fluttering of one or more of the small 'peaks'. For the time being, though, we will ignore this minor effect.
3. Finally, and this is the really important point at the moment, any repetitive wave can be analysed into a *fundamental* frequency and *harmonics*.

The last statement needs some clarification. By the term *fundamental* we mean the lowest frequency present. Then *harmonics* are frequencies which are *multiples* of the fundamental frequency.

To take simple numbers, suppose we have a note whose fundamental frequency is 120 Hz. This frequency will determine the *pitch* – at least very closely – and as a matter of interest will be close to B, just over an octave below middle C. Unless the sound is a very pure one, produced by electronic means, it will contain harmonics and these will have frequencies which are multiples of 120 Hz, thus:

120 Hz   fundamental
240 Hz   2nd harmonic
360 Hz   3rd harmonic
480 Hz   4th harmonic
600 Hz   5th harmonic, and so on

Notice that the *n*th harmonic has a frequency *n* times that of the fundamental. (It has sometimes been the practice to label the harmonics as 1st, 2nd and 3rd, etc. instead of 2nd, 3rd and 4th. The logic here is that *twice* fundamental frequency is the *first* harmonic. However, the system above, which is universal in the UK, makes the arithmetic easier. The tenth harmonic of A = 440 is 4400 Hz.)

It is important, in any sound recording and reproducing system, that the full range of harmonics should be present. For example, the highest notes normally met in music have fundamental frequencies of around 4 kHz, but their harmonics may easily go up to and even beyond the full limits of the audible range.

Figure 4.3 A square wave

In principle, any steady (i.e. repetitive) waveform can be *synthesized* by combining in the correct proportions all the necessary harmonics – not too difficult a task with modern electronics, although the costs of producing more than, say, ten or so harmonics may not be worthwhile. A particularly interesting example is a *square* wave (Figure 4.3). This can be shown to consist of an infinite number of the *odd-numbered* harmonics, having their amplitudes in the series:

1 unit of fundamental
⅓ unit of 3rd harmonic
⅕ unit of 5th harmonic
⅐ unit of 7th harmonic, and so on

It takes upwards of 20 components (around the 41st harmonic or higher) to produce a reasonable square wave, so that to produce a 1000 Hz square wave means having frequencies of at least 40 kHz.

An interesting, and not too difficult, exercise with a home computer is to write a program in BASIC which will plot square waves starting with only the fundamental and third harmonic and then adding other harmonics in their correct proportions.

A further aspect of harmonics is what is called 'false bass'. We've said that the ear bases its estimate of pitch on the fundamental – the lowest frequency present. This, although true most of the time, is not always correct. It is possible to suppress the fundamental and perhaps one or two of the lowest harmonics, and yet the ear will still base its perception of pitch on the fundamental frequency, although this is missing! It appears that the brain uses the spacing of the harmonics to 'calculate' the fundamental. For example, given harmonics of 300, 400, 500 and 600 Hz, the spacing of 100 Hz is the most probable fundamental frequency. The salvation of many cheap radios and cassette players, where the loudspeaker is too small to reproduce low frequencies, lies in the brain's ability to 'insert' the lost fundamentals. The oboe is an interesting instrument from this point of view. Its note contains virtually no fundamental nor the 2nd and 3rd harmonics – but its pitch is that of the missing fundamental.

Timbre (pronounced 'tarmbre')

By this we mean the individual quality of a sound – that which distinguishes, say, a trumpet from a clarinet. At one time it was thought that it was simply the number and relative intensities of the harmonics that determined the timbre of a sound but in the last few decades it has been realized that this is only partly true. What is very important is the nature of the *start* of the sound. Any musical note begins with a number of frequencies which are not related to the fundamental. These die away over several cycles, leaving the steady waveform with its harmonics. For some reason the ear attaches great importance to these short-lived frequencies, called the *starting transients*, to such an extent that if they are missing or distorted it may sometimes be very difficult to identify the instrument. A possibly extreme case is that of the flute and trumpet. In some circumstances it may be impossible to distinguish between them if the first second or two of their notes are masked by, for example, a further loud noise. The significance of the starting transients cannot be overstated. We shall refer to them several times later on.

The fallibility of the ear

The ear, as we have said, is remarkably sensitive; it also has great acuity – that is it can detect subtle changes in the nature of a sound, generally far better than any scientific instrument. Unfortunately it can also be easily fooled!

To begin with we tend to hear what we want to hear, and what we can see can sometimes influence our hearing also. Some years ago the author tried an experiment of getting groups of experienced listeners to judge an array of different loudspeakers and make notes giving each loudspeaker a rating. Each group made its assessment twice – once when the members could see the loudspeakers and once when the loudspeakers were hidden behind very thin and acoustically transparent muslin curtains. The ratings were almost always very different when the listeners couldn't see the loudspeakers! Most people who have worked in sound will know that one can make an adjustment to a control and sit back, well satisfied with the adjustment, only to find later that the adjustment had been to a control that wasn't in circuit! It also may come as a surprise to find that the average person's ability to remember sounds *really accurately* lasts for perhaps a second or two. And, as a final illustration, about four out of five people, when played a stereo recording of aircraft over good loudspeakers and in decent listening conditions, find that there appears to be a height component to the sound. That is, if the sound image goes from, say, left to right most people find that the image also rises well above the line of the loudspeakers – possibly even almost overhead. This can be a particularly powerful illusion. The author and a colleague once made some stereo recordings of low-flying aircraft. On listening to replays we both found this height effect, although we both knew that the angle the aircraft had subtended at the microphones had been much less than the apparent height in the listening room. No effort of will could ever bring the images down to their 'correct' height!

The ability of the ear to fool itself is something that everyone concerned with sound should always be aware of.

5 Room acoustics

This chapter deals with various aspects of what are often called 'room acoustics'. We shall take the word 'room' to mean almost any enclosure with a floor, ceiling and four (or more) walls. Mostly we should have at the back of our minds that we are thinking less about domestic sitting rooms than about studios for television, radio and recording. Concert halls could also come under this heading.

There are three main aspects of room acoustics:

1. The sound insulation needed. This obviously depends very much on the purpose of the 'room'. We shall look at some requirements and outline the ways in which satisfactory insulation is achieved.
2. The nature of 'room resonances' and how they can be minimized.
3. Reverberation time – that is, the decay of sound in the room.

Sound insulation

Basically this usually means keeping external noises out, but total silence is impracticable because there is also the problem of noise generally *within* the studio. The first thing to consider, of course, is what noise level is permissible. People often talk cheerfully about 'sound-proofed rooms', but full sound proofing is likely to be prohibitively expensive, so to be realistic one has to see what background level can be tolerated. Some permissible background noise levels are given in Table 5.1.

Table 5.1 Permissible noise levels

Environment	Permissible noise level (dBA)
Hospital ward	45
Large retail store	50–55
Open-plan office	45
Classroom	35–45
Living room (urban house)	40

Broadcasting and recording studios need slightly fuller explanations. *Radio studios* are often the most critical areas in terms of their acoustics as, unlike television studios, the 'picture' has to be painted entirely by sounds. Intrusive noises can thus totally destroy the illusion which is being created. This is especially true of radio drama studios, where the background noise level must be as low as possible. A figure of 15–20 dBA is fairly representative. (Note that the self-generated electrical noise in microphones is of the order of 15 dBA, so there is little point in trying to make studios much quieter than this.)

Studios for music, whether broadcasting or recording, can be more permissive, depending on the type of music. Rock bands are usually loud enough to drown quite a lot of external noise, but this shouldn't be used as an excuse for poor studio design – there are times when things have to be very quiet. Orchestral music needs low background noise levels because there are frequently bars of silence. For this reason it might appear that conditions should be as stringent as they are for radio drama. However, designers have to be realistic, which means recognizing the fact that a hundred or so musicians cannot be utterly silent. Chairs may creak, however faintly, pages of music are turned, and so on.

Television studios have less strict requirements. The reason for this is that total silence in a television studio is an impossibility. Quite apart from anything else the ventilation system almost always generates a slight whisper (or worse, sometimes) and actors, cameras and crew members have to move around. Fortunately, because viewers can *see* what is happening, their brains make allowances and can usually push into a lower level of consciousness noises which would be unacceptable in radio. Reasonable background noise levels in studios are shown in Table 5.2.

Note that radio studios can be acoustically designed for particular functions. Television studios are far too costly to be anything other than 'general purpose', except for relatively small studios used for things like news – and even they may have to accommodate different types of programme.

Broadly there are two categories of external sounds. These are

- Airborne sound
- Structure-borne sound

Table 5.2 Studio background noise levels

Studio	Acceptable noise level (dBA)
Radio drama	20
Radio orchestral music	25
Radio pop music	30
Television studio	30

Airborne sound

By *airborne* we mean that the sound waves have travelled through the air for the vast majority of their journey. External sound entering a conventional room will probably have travelled through the glass of the windows, but we couldn't take that small distance into account in describing the type of progress. We'd still call it airborne sound. The effects of airborne sound can be greatly reduced by some or all of the following:

1. All walls (and ceilings, if necessary) should have as much mass per unit surface area as possible. The relationship between sound insulation effect (that is, the difference in sound pressure levels on the two sides of the wall) and mass/unit area is given in the so-called mass law, shown in Figure 5.1. Notice that doubling the mass/unit area increases the sound insulation by between 4 and 6 dB. We are making the assumption that the wall is large and that there is no sound leakage round the sides, over the top or through doors and windows. Also the frequency of the sound plays a big part. With most materials the insulation is much less at low frequencies than at high frequencies.

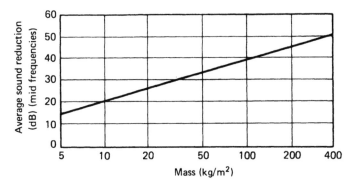

Figure 5.1 The mass law

Nevertheless, to give some indication of practicalities, a single-thickness brick wall (100 mm thick) will have on average a sound insulation of about 45 dB. This increases to around 50 dB with a double thickness (200 mm) of brick.

Mass, however, isn't the only way of achieving insulation. Good results can be obtained by using several separated layers of relatively light material (plasterboard for example.) Provided the layers are not in direct contact with each other the insulation can be much better than a single skin of equivalent mass.

2. Windows must be double- or triple-glazed. The spacings here are very different from those which are usually used for *thermal* insulation, where the two sheets of glass are several millimetres apart. Sound insulation needs glass separations of about 200 mm – not practicable for domestic thermal insulation. (When prospective customers are invited to consider having their homes double-glazed sound insulation is often quoted as a further benefit. There usually *is* an advantage, but it comes about almost entirely because there is a double weight (mass per unit area) of glass. Also any gaps and leaks are sealed – see below. The air space between the sheets of glass in domestic double glazing generally does little to keep sound out!)
3. All gaps and cracks *must* be sealed. Sound waves have an uncanny knack of finding small crevices and going through them. Sometimes it is no easy matter tracing small crevices through which external noises are passing. Places where services such as water and electrical circuits enter are often culprits. For good sealing of doors, studios usually make use of what is called a 'magnetic' seal – a system of magnets in a flexible plastic fitted to all edges of the door. When the door closes they attract strips of steel which are in a similar flexible material fixed to the door jambs and sill.

Structure-borne sound

By this we mean sound that travels, at least for the great majority of its journey, as vibrations in the fabric of the building. Unfortunately most building materials, concrete, steel and brick for instance, are very good conductors of vibration. One has only to have heard the effect of someone using a power drill to make a hole in any part of a house to appreciate this fact. Part of the trouble is because there are usually many parallel (*flanking*) paths. Figure 5.2 illustrates this. Vibrations starting at A have many paths available to them to get to B – the idea of resistors

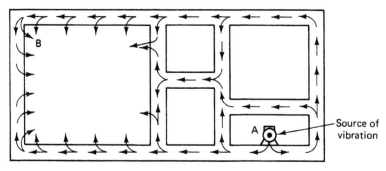

Figure 5.2 Structure-borne sound

in parallel in an electrical circuit is a reasonable analogy. There are various courses of action available to acoustic designers:

1. The most obvious is to avoid having any significant source of vibration in the building.
2. Where there is machinery, such as a lift motor, this should be mounted on resilient supports.
3. In studio centres it is usual to mount the studios themselves on resilient supports, such as steel springs or sheets of some type of rubber. When this is done it is of course necessary to make sure that adjoining corridors and offices are carefully isolated – the tie rods joining the studio walls with other walls must be slightly resilient, and so on.
4. Offices can be carpeted and corridors may have special resilient floor coverings.

The reduction of structure-borne sound is almost always a very expensive business. It can be achieved in a specially designed building, but it is almost impossible to do anything much in an existing building – except stop the offending machinery during recordings!

Room resonances

If a sound is generated between two non-absorbent parallel walls it, or at least some of it, will be reflected to and fro from wall to wall until it eventually dies away. Let us suppose that in Figure 5.3 there is a small loudspeaker emitting a steady tone of frequency f. This will have a wavelength of $\lambda = c/f$. If it so happens that the wall separation l is an integral number of half wavelengths then an acoustic resonance occurs. The energy builds up until the losses (at the walls and in the air) equal the energy emitted by the loudspeaker. The simplest mode

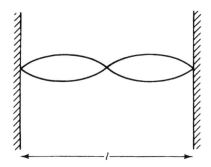

Figure 5.3 Room resonances

of resonance is the one when $l = \frac{1}{2}\lambda$. Others can occur when $l = \lambda$, $l = 1\frac{1}{2}\lambda$, $l = 2\lambda$, $l = 2\frac{1}{2}\lambda$, and so on. A formula for calculating these resonant frequencies is:

$$f = \frac{nc}{2l}$$

where $n = 1, 2, 3$, etc.

It is not difficult to detect these in most rooms if a steady tone can be reproduced from a loudspeaker. By stopping up one ear and moving about, the volume of sound will usually be found to vary fairly markedly. The pattern of maxima and minima will not usually be as clear as in Figure 5.3 because there are likely to be disturbances caused by resonances between the other parallel surfaces. An arrangement of these maxima and minima in a resonant condition is known as a *standing wave pattern*, which is not a very good term because the waves are not stationary. The maxima and minima are in fixed positions, true, but a wave *cannot* have a fixed or stationary position!

What we have in Figure 5.3 are graphs of *particle displacement* – plots of the movement of the air particles. A brief reference was made to particle displacement in Chapter 1 (Longitudinal waves), when it was pointed out that *pressure* graphs are usually much more useful. One possible exception to this occurs when we meet standing waves. Notice, in Figure 5.3, that there is a *displacement minimum* at the walls. This is, after all, what one should expect – the air particles cannot move into the wall, nor can they move away leaving a vacuum. Air particle movement is greatest at a distance $\frac{1}{4}\lambda$ from the wall. If we think about *pressure* graphs we ought to expect there to be maxima at the walls, and this is what happens. Figure 5.4 shows standing waves drawn as pressure graphs. It also introduces new terms; instead of maxima there are *antinodes* and for minima there are *nodes*. (The word node comes from the Latin and it means

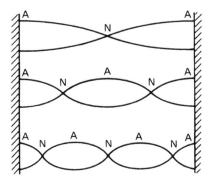

Figure 5.4 Standing waves – pressure graphs. A = antinode; N = node

'knot'. In general mathematical and scientific senses it means a crossing point.)

We are now in a position to think what happens if there are standing waves in a studio. Microphones, as we shall later see, depend primarily for their operation on the pressures in a sound wave. Imagine a microphone placed a distance x from the left-hand wall in Figure 5.4. It will be at a node for certain frequencies and an antinode for others, and at some intermediate condition for yet other frequencies. The sound that it picks up will not be a true version of the original. What is more, its output will depend very much on where the microphone is between the walls. Standing waves in a studio are therefore to be avoided. Before we go on to see how this is done, and it is in principle not difficult, we should point out that the diagrams of standing waves we have shown are very much simplified. Any room or studio has at least four walls, some pairs being more or less parallel to each other, while the floor and ceiling will also probably be parallel. There are thus going to be standing waves between *all* pairs of parallel surfaces, and, as if that were not enough, they can also occur between opposite *edges* – where walls meet floors for example, and between opposite *corners*. It is possible, although rather tedious, to calculate all these standing waves, or room resonances (the terms can be taken as meaning the same thing). Lord Rayleigh (1842–1919), who did a great deal of work on the mathematics and theory of sound, has had his name given to a formula for calculating all these resonant frequencies:

$$f = \frac{c}{2} \sqrt{\left(\frac{p}{l}\right)^2 + \left(\frac{q}{w}\right)^2 + \left(\frac{r}{h}\right)^2}$$

where p, q and r are integers (0, 1, 2, 3, etc.), c is our old friend the velocity of sound, and l, w and h are the length, width and height of the room.

Notice that if q and r are both 0 so that p is 1, 2, 3 and so on, this gives us exactly the simple frequencies for a pair of parallel walls as in Figure 5.3. And the addition of squared terms, with an overall square root, is applying Pythagoras' theorem to account for the diagonal resonances.

We said a little earlier that minimizing standing waves is, in principle, not too difficult. To begin with, any sound absorption will reduce the amount of reflection and hence the size of the antinodes in relation to the nodes. The other practical answer is to have irregularities in the various surfaces. Irregularities provide *diffusion* – the breaking-up of the reflected waves. Radio studios commonly have sound-absorbent boxes fitted to walls. Besides providing absorption (a topic we will deal with a little later) they can also provide diffusion. In recording studios an attractive decor may actually be providing the necessary diffusion, while in television studios the sets (scenery) and technical equipment such as large lights may provide enough diffusion. A large concert hall is likely to have many irregularities – boxes for the expensive seats, non-parallel surfaces and ceilings with deep recesses ('coffering'). To break up the reflected sound the irregularities must be relatively large. Their depth should be not less than about one-seventh of the longest wavelengths, ideally. (This may not be practicable.)

In recent years some studios have made use of things called Quadratic Residue Diffusers. Their theory is rather complex but it boils down to giving better break-up of sound reflectors from numbers of surfaces whose depth varies in an approximately random fashion.

A third way of reducing the worst effects of standing waves lies in the hands of the architect: avoiding simple mathematical relationships between the room dimensions. The worst possible case is that of a room which is a cube. All the wall-to-wall and floor-to-ceiling frequencies will be the same, the edge-to-edge ones will be the same, and the corner-to-corner ones will be the same.

A final point about standing waves in rooms: without going to the trouble of using the Rayleigh formula above we can learn something about the distribution of resonances from the simple formula we met earlier for calculating the resonant frequencies between a pair of parallel walls:

$$f = \frac{nc}{2l}$$

Taking c as 340 m/s and l, a typical room dimension, as 10 m, we find that resonances will occur at 17 Hz, 34 Hz, 51 Hz, 68 Hz, 85 Hz, . . . , 170 Hz, 187 Hz, 204 Hz, and so on. Two observations:

1. The lowest resonances are within the range of normal hearing (only just, in the case of 17 Hz).
2. The first two frequencies are an octave apart; as we go higher up the range the spacing between the resonances becomes, in musical terms, very much less. 204 Hz and 187 Hz are about $1\frac{1}{2}$ semitones apart.

Now let's take a much bigger wall spacing of 30 m – perhaps the length of a large television studio. The resonant frequencies are now 5.7 Hz, 11.3 Hz, 17 Hz, 22.7 Hz, 28.3 Hz, 34 Hz, 39.7 Hz, . . . Again, two observations:

1. As before, the first two frequencies are an octave apart, but they are so low in frequency that they will be inaudible.
2. By the time we get into the audible range the resonances are, in musical terms, fairly close together.

What this all means is that standing waves, if they are going to occur, are much more of a nuisance, by being identifiable, in small rooms than in large ones. This is often a major reason for the 'boxy' acoustics of small rooms such as bathrooms.

6 Reverberation

Reverberation time

In any room (and remember that we are using the word 'room' to mean *any* enclosure with walls, floor and ceiling) sounds do not die away instantly. A sound produced inside the room spreads out to the various surfaces and is reflected repeatedly from one surface to another, albeit with a loss of energy at each reflection. Eventually, after possibly a very large number of reflections, the sound dies to inaudibility. Figure 6.1 illustrates this process, called *reverberation*.

An immediate question is likely to be, how long does it take for the reverberation to die to inaudibility? The first person to try to provide an answer was the American physicist W. C. Sabine who, towards the end of the 19th century, carried out a notable series of experiments. Using an organ pipe driven by a constant-pressure air supply as a source of sound, he trained himself and his assistants to detect when the sound pressure at their ears had fallen to one-millionth of the original. Sabine coined the term *reverberation time* and his definition involved a decay in pressure of a million to one. Now we talk of a decay through 60 dB as that is equivalent to a pressure change of a million to one.

Reverberation time, RT for short (sometimes T_{60} is used), is defined as *the time taken for the sound in a room to decay through 60 dB*. Figure 6.2 shows this diagrammatically. Notice that the decay curve is now shown as a straight line –

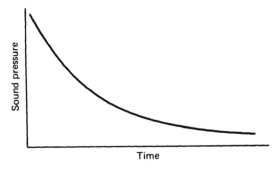

Figure 6.1 Reverberation

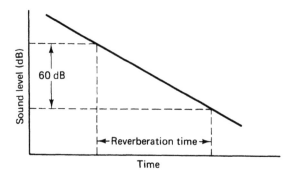

Figure 6.2 Reverberation time

this is a consequence of using decibels for the vertical scale instead of units of pressure. The decay of sound pressure in an ideal case follows what mathematicians call an *exponential* curve. It has a logarithmic characteristic and it follows the same decay curve as a cooling substance or a radio-active material. The decay curve in Figure 6.2 has been simplified, by the way. In reality such curves have fluctuations, especially near the lower end.

Primarily reverberation time is affected by two things:

1. The amount of sound absorptive material in the room – we shall look at absorption in more detail below.
2. The size of the room. The bigger the room the longer it will take the sound waves to travel between reflections. Since it is mainly by reflection that energy is lost it follows that in a big room, other things being equal, the reverberation time will be longer than in a small room. In fact, RT ∝ room volume.

Sound absorption

All materials absorb sound to some extent. (Note, by the way, absorber but absorption.) Hard, inflexible substances with shiny surfaces may absorb very little. Porous materials on the other hand can be very effective absorbers. The term *absorption coefficient* is used as a measure of absorbent properties. Absorption coefficient, which we will denote by a, is defined as

$$\frac{\text{Amount of sound energy absorbed}}{\text{Total incident sound energy}}$$

Thus a perfect reflecting material would have a value of $a = 0$; a perfect absorber would have $a = 1$.

Table 6.1 Absorption coefficients

	125 Hz	500 Hz	4000 Hz
Brick wall	0.02	0.03	0.07
Unplastered breeze blocks	0.25	0.60	0.45
Heavy drape curtains	0.1	0.4	0.5
Parquet floor	0.05	0.06	0.022
1 cm thick carpet	0.09	0.21	0.37

To complicate matters, a generally varies with frequency; most substances are better absorbers at high frequencies than at low. The section on porous absorbers explains why. Table 6.1 gives values of a for a few well-known substances. A seated person is equivalent to roughly half a square metre of perfect absorber, or one square metre of absorber having $a = 0.5$.

Sabine's formula

Sabine found that there was a relationship between volume (V), absorption and reverberation time:

$$RT \text{ (seconds)} = \frac{0.16\,V}{S_1 a_1 + S_2 a_2 + S_3 a_3 + \ldots}$$

where S_1 is the area whose absorption coefficient is a_1, etc.

Suppose we have a wall whose dimensions are 5×8 m so that its area is $40\,\text{m}^2$. If the average a for the wall were 0.4, then Sa for the wall would be $40 \times 0.4 = 16$ units. These units are called *sabines* after the pioneer of practical acoustics (1 sabine $= 1\,\text{m}^2$ of perfect absorber, $a = 1.0$).

We could write Sabine's formula slightly differently:

$$RT = \frac{0.16\,V}{\text{Total number of sabines}} \text{ seconds}$$

It might seem as if this were a useful formula for calculating values of reverberation time. In fact it isn't much use! The trouble is that in any real room there are so many types of material that it is very difficult to find out all their values of a at different frequencies. Also, the effective value of a is often dependent on whether the material is in one large area or whether it is dispersed. It is possible to do *rough* calculations, but accurate ones are almost impossible, as well as tedious. In practice reverberation times are measured. A suitably loud noise – generally a warbling tone to avoid exciting too many standing waves – is produced from a loudspeaker and a microphone records the decay of the sound after the noise is switched off. Fairly complex microprocessor circuitry is usually needed to average out the measurements made at several different microphone positions in the room.

Where the Sabine formula *is* useful is for calculating how much absorption is needed to give a particular value of reverberation time. For example, the bare shell of a studio might have a reverberation time of 5 or 6 seconds, or maybe more. If the desired reverberation time is, say, 1.5 seconds then, given the dimensions of the studio, it isn't difficult to calculate how many sabines of absorber are going to be needed. It must be added, though, that the answer is not likely to be very accurate! In practice a fair amount of adjustment is needed when the absorbent material is in place.

The Sabine formula is reasonably accurate when the amount of absorption is small. The reader might care to work out the reverberation time for a room of whatever dimensions he or she chooses, giving *all* walls, floor and ceiling a covering with 100% effective absorber ($a = 1.0$). Common sense says that the reverberation time will be zero, but the calculation doesn't come to this. There is a modified form of Sabine's formula known as the Eyring formula which gives a more accurate result:

$$RT = \frac{0.16\,V}{-S\log_e(1-a')}$$

where S is the total area of all surfaces and a' is the average absorption coefficient.

A further refinement is to allow for absorption by the air. This is usually insignificant below a few kilohertz, and in small rooms, but may be important in large halls and studios. An additional term of $+kV$ is put on to the bottom line; V is, again, the volume and k is a number which depends on frequency and the relative humidity of the air, being largest in dry air and also increasing with frequency.

Optimum reverberation times

There is no simple law which allows us to calculate what the reverberation time should be for any particular room, studio or concert hall. There are preferred figures, but these arise from custom, practice and history rather than any scientific study. Let's look at a few examples:

Average domestic sitting room. This probably has a reverberation time of around half a second, although no one seems to have carried out a proper survey.

Churches.   Because of their large volume and tendency to have non-absorbent stone walls and floor most churches of any size have reverberation times of a few seconds at low frequencies, the reverberation time dropping as the frequency rises, partly because of the air absorption we mentioned above. Large cathedrals may have reverberation times at low frequencies of as much as 12 seconds, while small chapels which have plastered (i.e. absorbent) walls may have quite short values – perhaps a second or so.

Concert halls.   Around two seconds, but falling at the higher frequencies, is fairly typical for the bigger halls. This figure arises from the large volumes and the use of traditional building materials.

An interesting point is that the 19th century was a peak era for building the major halls. Because a lot of noise was needed to fill them the large symphony orchestra developed, replacing to some extent the small chamber orchestras of the previous century. Consequently composers from Beethoven onwards wrote their music to be heard in such halls and with two-second reverberation times. It follows that such orchestral music doesn't usually sound at its best unless the reverberation time is around two seconds. This influences the design of music studios and artificial reverberation devices.

Studios for orchestral music.   Radio and recording studios for orchestral music ideally should have reverberation times of about two seconds if they are to simulate the conditions of a large concert hall. In practice, because such studios have to be much smaller than the average concert hall (for economic reasons), many have reverberation times less than two seconds. Here good microphone placing and artificial reverberation devices come to the rescue.

Studios for chamber music.   Much traditional chamber music was written to be played and heard in medium-sized and often richly furnished rooms where the reverberation time was relatively short – perhaps one second. For this reason the ideal studio for this type of music should have a corresponding reverberation time.

Studios for rock-type music.   For reasons which are very different from the ones above the reverberation time for these studios needs to be short – as short as possible, perhaps. Half a second is typical. This is because multi-microphone techniques are usually used, with one microphone for each instrument as the norm. The important thing here is that there is as little 'spill' as possible. In other words there should be minimal reflection from walls, etc. so that each microphone picks up as little as possible of the other instruments. With minimal reflection – maximum absorption – the reverberation time is short.

Radio studios for speech.   The usual aim here is to make the voice that comes out of the listener's loudspeaker sound reasonably close; perhaps in the same room. Too long a reverberation time gives an impression of remoteness; too short a reverberation time makes the voice sound unnaturally 'dry'. It is also rather unpleasant for the speaker. A figure of about 0.4 second is usually regarded as acceptable as a reverberation time for talks studios, although the type of microphone and the distance at which it is placed from the speaker can have substantial modifying effects.

Radio drama studios.   These need to provide more than one acoustic environment: a very short reverberation time to simulate the open air (around 0.1–0.2 second), a medium reverberation time of perhaps half a second for domestic situations, and a rather longer reverberation time (nearer one second) for what would be 'lively' acoustics in real life, church interiors for example. An obvious question is, why not use artificial reverberation to simulate reverberant conditions? The answer briefly is that artificial systems may well be needed, but actors generally need some reverberation in the studio to help them react to the imaginary environment. Consequently a radio drama studio will generally be divided into various areas, each with a different reverberation time.

Television studios.   Full-size studios need to be used for all types of music, for speech and for drama. In other words we have an almost impossible requirement! (It's too expensive to have studios dedicated to particular purposes, as in radio. To help, though, the person at home can *see* what's happening and this often, to some extent, compensates for minor defects in the studio acoustics.) A possible answer might be to make all television studios acoustically very 'dead' – i.e. have short reverberation times – and then liven them up with artificial means. Unfortunately this is generally not possible. A television studio has to have a very hard, and therefore reflective, floor so that cameras can be moved about smoothly. Also there have to be panels on the walls where microphones, cameras and other equipment can be plugged in. These are also non-absorbent. As a result there is so much sound-reflective area that it is almost impossible to make a television studio have a short reverberation time. Typical values range from about 0.7 to 1.1 second.

The reader might find it a worthwhile experience to verify this. Take the dimensions of the studio as 30 m long, 25 m wide and 15 m high. Assume that the floor has an absorption coefficient of zero and take the average a for all the other surfaces as 0.7 (fairly realistic). With relatively large absorptions the Sabine formula is, we know, not very accurate but it will be good enough to make the point. The answer will be found to be about 1 second. (The Eyring formula gives roughly three-quarters of a second.)

Theatres.   These generally have reverberation times of about 1 second. This is short enough to give reasonable intelligibility of speech.

Sound absorbers

The job of any sound absorber is to reduce air particle movement by friction. There is a range of commercially available absorbers – often in the form of some sort of tile which can be fitted to ceilings, walls, etc. Here we will only concern ourselves with the basic principles of sound absorption; commercial absorbers are based on these principles.

Porous absorbers

A layer of almost any porous or fibrous material will have a sound-absorbent effect. However, the layer has to be about $\frac{1}{4}\lambda$ thick to be very effective. Figure 6.3 shows what happens when a sound wave is reflected from a wall.

This is a *displacement* graph (see page 36). Notice that the displacement *antinode*, a point of maximum particle movement, is $\frac{1}{4}\lambda$ from the wall. This means that unless the absorber is thick enough to contain that antinode the loss of sound wave energy by friction will probably not be very great, although in practice it is sometimes found that good absorption occurs when the thickness is less than $\frac{1}{4}\lambda$. The fact that many sound waves will be striking the absorber at

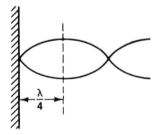

Figure 6.3 Particle displacement at reflection

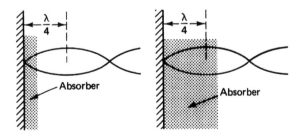

Figure 6.4 Operation of a porous absorber: (a) Absorber thickness $<\frac{1}{4}\lambda$, little absorption; (b) Absorber thickness $>\frac{1}{4}\lambda$, maximum absorption

oblique angles helps to make the overall absorption better than the diagrams imply.

For general use porous absorbers clearly have their limitations. If we wanted to absorb sound at 30 Hz (the lower end of the frequency range for general broadcasting and recording) we would need to have the absorbent material 1–2 m thick! However, if we were concerned only with absorption above, say, 500 Hz then $\frac{1}{4}\lambda$ is 17 cm, which is far more manageable, especially as in practice 10 cm might well be enough.

Very many materials can be porous absorbers, but not many of them are entirely acceptable, for various reasons. Cotton wool would do well but it is a fire risk; asbestos is also a hazard; glassfibre is undesirable because small particles can drift into the air. Porous plaster can work well but cannot easily be applied in the necessary thicknesses, and so on. Fortunately there are good materials, some of them based on types of mineral wool, and these are used extensively.

In some instances it has been found useful to have an airspace behind the absorber (Figure 6.5). This arrangement is often as effective as the full thickness of absorber because it still 'traps' the antinodes for the longer wavelengths, and only half the amount of material is needed.

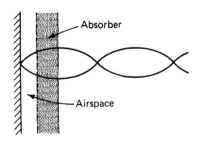

Figure 6.5 Porous absorber with airspace

Finally, the performance of a porous absorber can depend very much on the covering. It is usual to have a more or less decorative facing of fabric, perforated hardboard, etc. The right choice of fabric can *add* to the absorption; the amount of perforation in the hardboard can affect the absorption at different frequencies.

Wide-band porous absorbers

Having made the point that porous absorbers need to be impractically thick to provide reasonably low-frequency absorption, we must mention briefly a porous absorber that can have quite modest thickness. The wide-band porous absorber

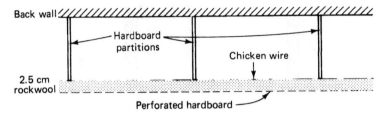

Figure 6.6 Wide-band porous absorber

was devised by BBC research engineers. Its construction is shown in Figure 6.6.

The characteristics depend to some extent on the overall thickness of the device and also on the type of perforated hardboard. A large proportion of perforation gives better high-frequency absorption; a small proportion is better at low frequencies. In general one can say that absorbers of this type can be effective from 60–70 Hz and above. They are widely used in BBC radio studios, where their modular construction can help to provide diffusion. There is no simple explanation of how the wide-band porous absorber works!

Panel absorbers

These are basically resonating systems. The 'panel' may be an area of plywood backed with an energy-absorbing material. Roofing felt and other similar bituminous substances are satisfactory. Behind the panel is an airspace which provides the 'spring' against which the mass of the panel vibrates. The device can be tuned to a particular frequency by adjusting the airspace behind the panel. The resonant frequency is given approximately by

$$f = \sqrt{\frac{60}{md}}$$

where m is the mass/area of the panel (kg/m^2) and d is the depth of the airspace (m).

Sometimes known as 'membrane' absorbers, panel absorbers can be used to give low-frequency absorption, when a number of panels tuned to slightly different frequencies in the required band are used. Alternatively they can be used to control particular troublesome frequencies.

Helmholtz resonators

Figure 6.7 illustrates the resonator named after Hermann von Helmholtz, German scientist, 1821–1894. Here the mass of the air m in the neck 'bounces' against the

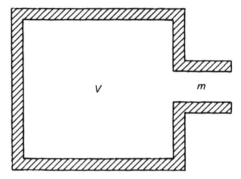

Figure 6.7 Basic Helmholtz resonator

spring (or compliance) provided by the volume of air V. Although the mass m may be very small the compliance provided by V is such that quite low resonant frequencies can occur in units of modest size. Easily obtainable examples are empty whisky or gin bottles, which usually resonate at about 100–120 Hz when the researcher blows across the top. The resonant frequency is approximately

$$f = \frac{c}{2\pi} \sqrt{\frac{A}{lV}}$$

where c is the velocity of sound, A is the cross-sectional area of the neck (m^2), l is the length of the neck (m) and V is the volume (m^3).

A feature of the Helmholtz resonator is that it can either absorb or re-radiate sound, depending on the friction in the neck. With a thin piece of gauze across the neck there is sufficient friction for there to be absorption, a fact which has been made use of in radio studios. An interesting use of Helmholtz resonators as re-radiators is in London's Royal Festival Hall. When the hall was built in the early 1950s it was found that the reverberation time was too short at low frequencies. About 90 Helmholtz resonators were fitted into the ceiling in a system which enhanced the reverberation time in this range. Each resonator contained a microphone, the output of which was amplified and fed to a loudspeaker at another point in the ceiling. The resonators were tuned at intervals of about 3 Hz to cover the range from 70 Hz to 340 Hz. The range was later extended to 168 resonators, covering the range 58–700 Hz. This system, known as *assisted resonance*, has been so successful that similar installations have been adopted in other halls in the UK, the United States and Eastern Europe.

Variable reverberation time systems

Assisted resonance, above, is an electronic method of enhancing RT. A number of ways exist of mechanically varying the reverberation time of a studio.

Basically, these consist of varying, usually by motors, the exposure of sound absorbent materials. Attempts to achieve this have been around for many years but until fairly recently they were not particularly successful, partly because of the difficulty of maintaining a desired RT vs frequency relationship.

7 Microphones

Any microphone can be thought of as having three essential components:

1. The diaphragm, which vibrates when sound waves strike it.
2. The transducer, which converts the diaphragm movements into electrical signals.
3. The casing, the design of which affects the characteristics of the microphone.

In fact the diaphragm is often an integral part of the transducer so we will look at the two together, under the heading of transducers. We will deal with the casing later in the chapter when we come to consider the directional characteristics of microphones.

Transducers

There are many ways in which vibrations caused by sound waves can be converted into electrical signals. One of the earliest to be used consisted of granules of carbon in contact with the diaphragm. As the latter vibrated the alternations of pressure on the carbon granules changed their electrical resistance. A current passing through the granules was thus made to vary in sympathy with the diaphragm movements. The so-called 'carbon microphone' was used very widely in telephones because of its relative cheapness, reliability and high output. It was also used in broadcasting in the 1930s, but was discarded after a few years when better microphone transducer systems became available. Its main drawback was that it generated a high level of background noise – a hiss apparently caused by minute electrical arcs between the granules.

Another transducer, still used in some cheap microphones, makes use of the *piezo-electric* effect. Slices of certain crystals (quartz is one such material) produce a small electromotive force (EMF) when the crystal slice is deformed. The 'crystal microphone' consists of a diaphragm connected to a suitable crystal system. However, this type of microphone can only operate on a metre or so of cable unless an amplifier is incorporated. This means that for serious use the crystal microphone becomes relatively expensive and then has no advantages over other types. (See under Electrostatic microphones for an explanation of why an amplifier is needed.)

The most widely used transducers used today are described below.

Moving-coil microphones

Figure 7.1 shows the construction of a moving-coil microphone. The *coil* typically consists of about 20 to 30 turns of wire. This is usually made of flattened aluminium – aluminium because of its lightness and flattened to make the thickness of the coil as small as possible, thus allowing the least possible gap

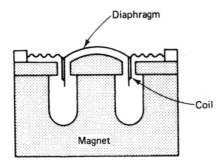

Figure 7.1 Moving-coil microphone

between the magnet poles. The diaphragm is domed in the centre, to make it rigid in this region, and corrugated at the outside to allow it to move to and fro. Movement of the coil generates an EMF which is proportional to velocity, flux density and length of conductor in the coil.

Facts about moving-coil transducers

1. The electrical impedance is around 30 ohms (some non-professional moving-coil microphones have a built-in step-up transformer to give a higher output. The impedance then is in the region of 20–100 kilohms).
2. With normal speech at a distance of about half a metre the output of a moving-coil microphone is likely to be rather less than 1 mV.
3. A big advantage can sometimes be that, unlike some other microphones, no electrical power is needed.
4. The coil and diaphragm assembly, although designed to have the least possible weight, is still rather heavier than the diaphragm in other microphones, and this means that the quality is rarely quite as good as with other systems.

5. Skilled labour is needed to make them and this has meant that they are no longer cheap devices.

Ribbon microphones

This is an excellent instance of the diaphragm (the ribbon) being actually part of the transducer. The ribbon is typically about 2 cm long and is very thin – about 0.00006 cm thick, which is of the same order as light wavelengths! The way in

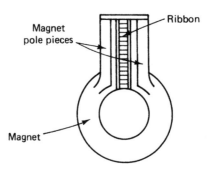

Figure 7.2 Ribbon microphone

which sound waves cause the diaphragm to move is slightly complex and we will look at this when we deal with directional properties.

Facts about ribbon transducers

1. The impedance of the ribbon is very small – less than 1 ohm. There is usually a transformer incorporated into the microphone and this changes the impedance at the output to around 30 ohms.
2. Because there is only one fairly short conductor to move to and fro in the magnetic field the microphone's sensitivity is low. Using normal speech at half a metre as our reference, the output of a ribbon microphone is likely to be about 0.1 mV.
3. The extreme lightness of the ribbon is an advantage in that the microphone's response to starting transients can be very good.
4. The ribbon is, however, very fragile. Practical microphones incorporate windshields which help to protect it (especially against those very unprofessional people who test a microphone by blowing at it!).

Electrostatic microphones

These are sometimes known as 'condenser' or 'capacitor' microphones. Again, the diaphragm is part of the transducer and is made usually of thin plastic on to which a thin layer of metal (sometimes gold) has been deposited. With the *back plate* it forms a capacitor having a value of around 20–30 pF ($1\,\text{pF} = 10^{-6}\,\mu\text{F}$). As the diaphragm vibrates the capacitance is varied slightly. The way in which an output is obtained is shown in Figure 7.4. The resistor R has a very high value

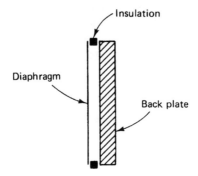

Figure 7.3 Electrostatic capsule

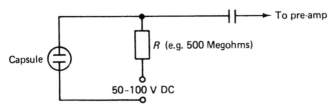

Figure 7.4 Basic circuitry of an electrostatic microphone

(hundreds of megohms), which is sufficient to ensure that the charge on the capacitor is 'locked in' so that it is effectively constant. Charge, capacitance and voltage are related by

$$Q = CV$$

so that if Q is constant and C varies then V must also vary.

Notice that an amplifier is referred to in Figure 7.4. This is because the impedance of the capsule is very high and, as with all high-impedance circuits, it is prone to trouble from induced voltages from other sources – mains hum being a very common offender. All audio circuits of any length, more than a metre or two, should be of *low impedance* if they are to carry low-level signals. The amplifier in the diagram ensures this – in fact to be accurate we should call it an 'impedance-changing amplifier' although it is almost always referred to in practice as a 'pre-amplifier'. (The impedance of a crystal microphone is also high, which is why we said in the section 'Transducers' that an amplifier was needed.)

The back plate in Figure 7.3 is shown as a solid piece of metal. In practice, since the small volume of air between the diaphragm and the back plate will not allow the diaphragm to vibrate easily, holes are drilled part-way into the plate to give a greater volume of air. These are known as 'blind' holes. Also, for reasons which will become clearer later (under *Cardioid* microphones, p. 61), the plate may be perforated with holes drilled right through it.

Facts about electrostatic transducers

1. The output impedance – after the amplifier – is typically in the range 150–250 ohms.
2. Because of the very high impedance of the capsule, insulation is vitally important. This means that damp can be a problem. Taking an electrostatic microphone from a cold environment (such as the boot of a car in winter) into a warm room can result in condensation, and until this dries off there are loud crackles, hisses and rumbles in the microphone's output. (The RF electrostatic microphone, outlined below, avoids this problem.)
3. The quality of output of an electrostatic microphone can be excellent.
4. A power supply is needed. This is not normally a problem as we shall see.

Electret and RF electrostatic microphones

A conventional electrostatic microphone needs a *polarizing* voltage, between the diaphragm and the back plate, of 50 V or more. This means that whatever is supplying power to the microphone needs to provide a low-voltage supply for the amplifier *and* a relatively high voltage for the capsule. However, certain materials exist which can be given a permanent electrostatic charge and they are known as *electrets* (by analogy with magnet). So, by using an electret material for either the diaphragm or the back plate the need for a polarizing voltage is removed (but there still needs to be a low-voltage supply for the amplifier). In all other respects an electret microphone is the same thing as the electrostatic microphone described above. There is a version of an electrostatic microphone which still has a capacitor as the capsule but uses it in an entirely different way. This is the *RF electrostatic* microphone. A simplified schematic diagram is shown in Figure 7.5.

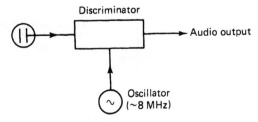

Figure 7.5 RF electrostatic microphone

In essence the system is like an FM transmitter/receiver combination, except that instead of a varying frequency being fed into the discriminator to give an audio output, here the frequency is constant and the changes in the capacitance of the capsule vary the tuning of the discriminator. In practice the circuitry is complex and expensive. The advantage is, though, that the system is almost entirely immune to the effects of condensation. Consequently the RF electrostatic principle is widely used in microphones which are to be used out of doors. (See Gun microphones, p. 65.)

Directional characteristics

Of great importance to the user is the way in which a particular microphone responds to sounds from different directions. As we shall soon see, this is where some aspects of the design of the microphone casing are important. There are five basic microphone *polar diagrams* (that is, graphical representations of the sensitivity of the microphone in different directions). We'll take these one at a time.

Omnidirectional microphones

Look at the simplified 'omni' microphone shown in Figure 7.6. The only way in which sound waves can get to the diaphragm is from the front. (In other types of

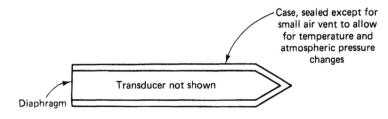

Figure 7.6 Basic omnidirectional microphone

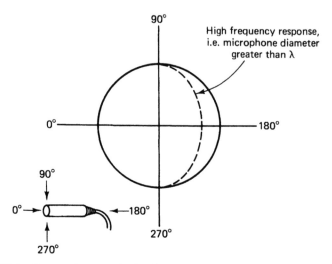

Figure 7.7 Polar diagrams for an omni microphone

microphone sound is allowed to reach both the front and the back of the diaphragm.) If the wavelength is *greater* than the microphone diameter we can assume that, because of diffraction, sound waves will strike the diaphragm no matter from which direction they arrive. The microphone will then have an *omnidirectional* (all directions) response, and we will represent this by a polar diagram which is a circle, as in Figure 7.7. If the sound wavelength is *smaller* than the microphone diameter then the diffraction process won't occur completely and waves from the back of the microphone will either not reach the diaphragm or, if they do, only partially. The dashed line in Figure 7.7 shows this.

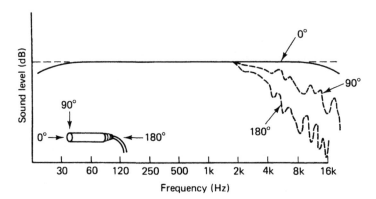

Figure 7.8 Typical frequency response graphs for an omni microphone

An alternative way of showing directional effects is by *frequency response graphs* at different frequencies. Figure 7.8 has been drawn for a typical omni microphone; here the omnidirectional characteristic is maintained up to about 2 kHz. As a rough guide the frequency above which there begins to be a departure from omnidirectional characteristics can be calculated in this way:

1. Find the microphone's diameter.

   Example: 2 cm.

2. Calculate the frequency for which this would be the wavelength.

   $f = 340 \, \text{m/s} \div 2 \, \text{cm} = 17 \, \text{kHz}$.

3. The microphone will be omnidirectional up to a frequency between 2 and 3 octaves below this, i.e. between a quarter and an eighth of the calculated figure.

   1 octave below is about 8 kHz; 2 octaves about 4 kHz; 3 octaves about 2 kHz. Take about 3 kHz as a near enough answer.

Facts about omnidirectional microphones

1. Most 'personal' microphones – those clipped to lapels, for instance – are omnis.
2. They are useful for hand-holding for interviews where they do not have to be pointed accurately at the speaker.
3. Compared with other microphones, they tend to be less prone to 'rumble' and also to the effects of wind-noise – but they still need windshields out of doors.

Figure-of-eight microphones

Figure 7.9 shows a microphone in which sound waves can reach *both* sides of the diaphragm. Sound waves arriving at the diaphragm from the left will obviously have the same effect as those arriving from the right. Those which come from the top or the bottom will pass the diaphragm with the same pressures on both sides of it, and there will be no resultant pressure on the diaphragm. It doesn't stretch the imagination too much to see that the microphone will have a polar diagram

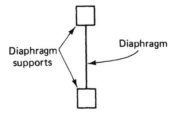

Figure 7.9 Basic figure-of-eight microphone

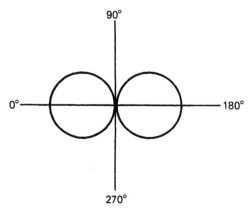

Figure 7.10 Figure-of-eight polar diagram

which is (a) symmetrical front-to-rear and (b) shows *no* output for sounds at right angles to the front-rear axis. In fact the polar diagram (called *figure-of-eight* or *bi-directional*) is as shown in Figure 7.10.

It may seem slightly odd that sound waves are allowed to strike both sides of the diaphragm. What happens is that there is actually a small pressure difference (gradient) between the two sides. Figure 7.11 shows this.

The point is that the waves reaching the rear of the diaphragm (assuming that wavelengths are large so that diffraction occurs) arrive there slightly later than waves striking the front. This time difference is very small: the actual extra distance travelled is typically of the order of 4 cm so the time difference is in the region of 0.1 ms. So, at any instant, the front and rear pressures on the diaphragm are out of phase by an amount corresponding to this small time. The vertical lines

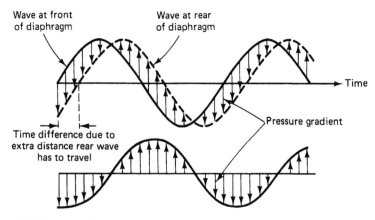

Figure 7.11 Pressure gradients

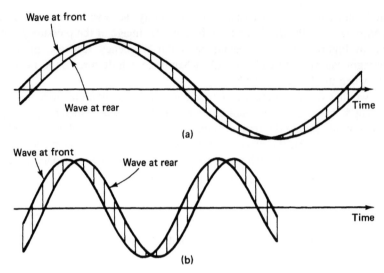

Figure 7.12 Pressure gradients at low and high frequencies: (a) low frequency; (b) high frequency

in Figure 7.11 thus represent the instantaneous pressure difference between the sides of the diaphragm, and it is this which results in the force causing the diaphragm to move.

There are, however, complications. Figure 7.12 represents the situation at (a) low frequencies and (b) a fairly high frequency – perhaps a few kilohertz. The vertical lines in Figure 7.12(a), representing the pressure gradient, are small; those in (b) are much greater, showing that the pressure gradient (and therefore the force on the diaphragm) rises with frequency. In Figure 7.13 the rise in pressure gradient with frequency is shown.

We would, of course, like our microphone to have a flat frequency response and this is far from flat. What designers of pressure gradient microphones do is to give the diaphragm a very low natural resonance frequency. If this and other

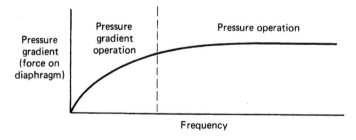

Figure 7.13 Pressure gradient against frequency

related mechanical characteristics are correctly achieved then the natural response curve of the diaphragm can be a mirror image of the pressure gradient curve in Figure 7.13. This results in a flat frequency response graph: the diaphragm can move to and fro easily when there is little force on it, rather less easily when the force is greater.

We would expect at some high frequency to have a condition where the sound wavelength was equal to the path difference and there would then be no pressure gradient at all. Taking the time difference as 0.1 ms, this would correspond to a frequency of 10 kHz, the wavelength being in practice about 4 cm. Fortunately this is small enough for diffraction round to the back of the diaphragm not to occur in any practical microphone.

Bass tip-up (proximity effect)

All pressure gradient microphones show what is known as *bass tip-up* or *proximity effect*. What this means is that when the source of sound is close to the microphone

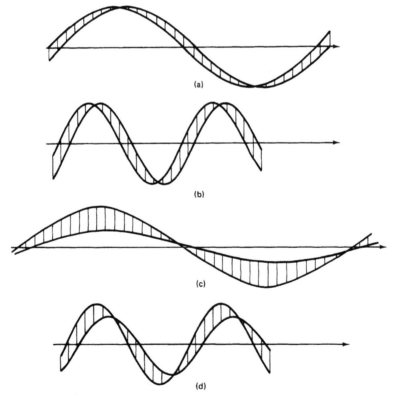

Figure 7.14 Bass tip-up: (a) Low frequency, distant source; (b) High frequency, distant source; (c) Low frequency, close source; (d) High frequency, close source

– less than about half a metre, typically – there is an exaggerated output of bass frequencies. A full explanation of this is rather complicated, but broadly, it is as follows. Figure 7.14(a) and (b) show what happens when the source of sound is a relatively long way away. We can assume that the extra 4 cm or so from front to back of the diaphragm is quite insignificant compared with the distance the sound has already travelled. Consequently inverse-square-law effects don't occur and the amplitudes of the front and rear waves are the same.

In Figure 7.14(c) and (d) the sound source is close, so that the rear wave is smaller in amplitude than the front wave. Comparison of the vertical lines, which represent the pressure gradient and hence the force on the diaphragm, shows that for close sources the low frequencies are boosted. This effect is made good use of in some microphones, especially what are known as *lip ribbon* microphones. These are hand-held microphones used widely for sporting commentaries. The microphone is positioned very close to the mouth – a bar is rested against the face between upper lip and nose to maintain the right spacing. The voice at this distance would be excessively 'bassy', but internal circuitry corrects this to give a reasonably flat response for the voice. More distant sounds, crowd noises for instance, will not have the bass tip-up but their low frequencies will still be affected by the circuitry. It is then possible to have intelligible speech from a commentator in circumstances where any other microphone would be virtually unusable.

Facts about pressure gradient microphones

1. Ribbon microphones lend themselves well to figure-of-eight operation.
2. Electrostatic microphones can be made to be figure-of-eight. We'll explain this later when we look at variable polar diagram microphones.
3. Because the diaphragm has a very low natural resonance frequency, pressure gradient microphones tend to be severely affected by vibration, rumble, etc.
4. A figure-of-eight polar diagram can sometimes be very useful in discriminating against unwanted sounds; the microphone is positioned so that they are to each side of the microphone.
5. The mathematical expression for a figure-of-eight microphone is

$r = \cos \theta$

r being the distance from the origin (where the horizontal and vertical axes intersect) at angle θ.

Cardioid microphones

Figure 7.15 shows a cardioid polar diagram. The word comes from the Greek meaning 'heart' (hence 'cardiac', 'cardiogram', etc.). A cardioid pattern has a definite mathematical formula:

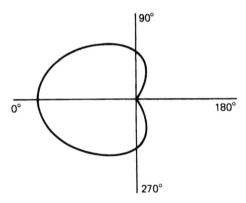

Figure 7.15 Cardioid polar diagram

$$r = 1 + \cos \theta$$

where r is the distance from the origin to the curve at angle θ. Now for an omni microphone, where the polar diagram is a circle, r is a constant. We could say that

$$r = 1 \tag{6.1}$$

For a figure-of-eight microphone we've said that

$$r = \cos \theta \tag{6.2}$$

Adding (6.1) and (6.2), we have

$$2r = 1 + \cos \theta$$

which is of the form of a cardioid. (The fact that we now have $2r$ instead of r doesn't alter the *shape* of the pattern.) With a scientific calculator and a few sheets of polar graph paper the reader can prove for him- or herself that these expressions really do give figures-of-eight and cardioids.

The inference then is that a cardioid microphone could be produced by combining an omni microphone and a figure-of-eight microphone. This in fact was the way that some early cardioids were made, but they were bulky and heavy, and the cardioid pattern wasn't generally very good. However, the point we are making is that some of the attributes of figure-of-eight microphones are carried on into cardioids, no matter what method is used to produce the pattern.

Also, because a cardioid is part omni, part figure-of-eight it is not surprising to find that this polar diagram can be obtained by allowing *some* sound to reach

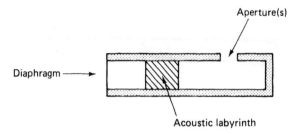

Figure 7.16 Simplified construction of a cardoid microphone

the rear of the microphone diaphragm (remember that in an omni microphone *no* sound reaches the rear while in a figure-of-eight there is *unrestricted* access to the rear). Inevitably, things are not quite as simple as that but Figure 7.16 gives an outline of the construction of a cardioid microphone.

The labyrinth can be thought of as causing a slight delay in the sound reaching the rear of the diaphragm. (It is also an *acoustic phase-shifting network* and cardioid microphones using this principle are often called 'phase shift' cardioids.) Incidentally, in an electrostatic cardioid, part of the labyrinth often consists of holes drilled right through the back plate.

Sounds which arrive from the front of the microphone, as in Figure 7.17(a), simply have a pressure gradient action on the diaphragm. Sounds coming from the rear (Figure 7.17(b)) have, if the labyrinth has been correctly designed, equal-length paths to front and rear of the diaphragm. They thus arrive on both sides at

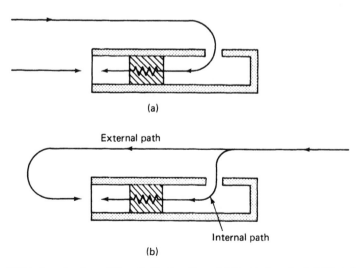

Figure 7.17 Action of a phase-shift cardioid microphone: (a) Sounds from front; (b) Sounds from rear

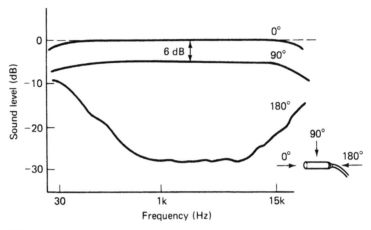

Figure 7.18 Frequency response graphs for a typical cardioid microphone

the same instant and can produce no resultant force. The microphone will not then give any output. That's the theory! In reality it is very difficult to get the labyrinth to operate like this over the whole of the audio range of frequencies. Figure 7.18 shows typical frequency response curves for a good cardioid microphone for sounds arriving from the front (0°), from the side (90°) and from the rear (180°). The *front-to-back separation*, as it is called, rarely exceeds about 30 dB. However, this is perfectly adequate for most professional purposes.

Facts about cardioid microphones

1. Because they have a partly pressure gradient operation they usually show some bass tip-up.
2. They also tend to be rather prone to vibration and rumble.
3. The vents allowing sound to enter to the rear of the diaphragm can be troublesome when the microphone is used out of doors because wind can create turbulence effects. Good windshielding is essential, and in some microphones this is built in.
4. The 'dead' area at the back can be very useful in discriminating against unwanted noises.

Hypercardioid microphones

Figure 7.19 shows a hypercardioid polar diagram. It is part-way between cardioid and figure-of-eight, having, theoretically, nulls at 45° off the rear axis. Many hypercardioids are constructed as a kind of cardioid but with greater sound wave access to the rear of the diaphragm.

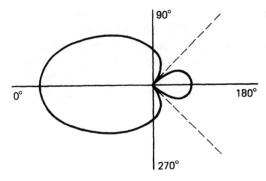

Figure 7.19 Hypercardioid polar diagram

Facts about hypercardioid microphones

1. It is sometimes useful to have two dead sides near the rear of the microphone.
2. The front lobe is slightly narrower than the lobe of a cardioid – this again is sometimes helpful.
3. Like all microphones which have a pressure-gradient component, hyper-cardioids tend to show the bass tip-up effect and they are also rather prone to pick up rumble and vibration, being usually worse than cardioid microphones in these respects.
4. Some short gun microphones (see below) are often described as having a hypercardioid polar diagram. This is not completely accurate, but in practice is not a seriously misleading statement.

Gun microphones

There are really two types of gun microphone, differing only in length. Their important characteristic is that they are very directional in their response.

The true gun microphones are metal tubes rather more than half a metre in length and with a diameter of about 2 cm. The tube is perforated or slotted along much of its length, as shown in Figure 7.20. The action of a gun microphone is based upon the fact that sound waves approaching from the axis along which the

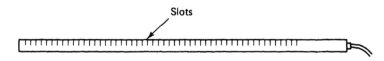

Figure 7.20 Gun microphone

gun is pointing can be assumed to enter the holes or slots and travel quite normally to the diaphragm. Those arriving at an angle will travel by different length paths to the diaphragm, depending on whether they enter the tube near the front or near the diaphragm. These differences in path length result in cancellation effects, partial if the wavelengths are greater than the length of the tube, more complete at shorter wavelengths. The resulting polar diagrams are shown in Figure 7.21.

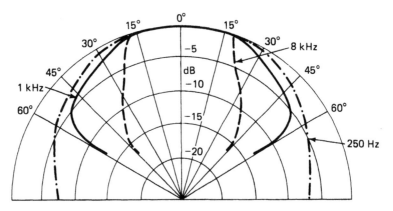

Figure 7.21 Polar diagrams for a typical gun microphone

One important thing to notice is that the cancellation process can only work if the sound wavelengths are comparable with, or less than, the slotted length of the tube. As a result gun microphones of practicable size are only very directional at frequencies above 3–4 kHz, when the angle of pick-up is in the region of ±15°. Theoretically a gun microphone ought to be virtually omnidirectional at low frequencies but this is avoided by making the capsule assembly a cardioid so that below, say, 100 Hz the microphone is still directional, although with a much wider angle of pick-up than at high frequencies.

The shorter gun microphones, where the slotted part of the tube is some 20–25 cm long, have a much wider angle of pick-up. They are sometimes described as being hypercardioids and this can be a fair statement in practice, at least up to about 2 kHz.

Facts about gun microphones

1. They are very extensively used for outside work – news gathering, location drama, and so on.
2. For this reason many gun microphones use the RF electrostatic principle described earlier.

3. The longer types tend not to work too well in ordinary rooms and small studios. It is possible for the directional properties to be little better than cardioid in these circumstances.
4. For outside work a windshield is essential.
5. They are occasionally fixed to cameras for coverage of sporting events.
6. It makes virtually no difference to the polar diagram whether the holes or slots are uppermost or facing down.

Variable polar diagram microphones

All the main polar diagrams, except for the highly directional gun type, can be produced in one electrostatic unit. There are several makes of *variable polar diagram* microphones and they all work in more or less the same way (Figure 7.22). The capsule consists of two electrostatic cardioids mounted back-to-back. In fact there are usually two diaphragms with a common back plate as Figure 7.22(b) shows.

(a)

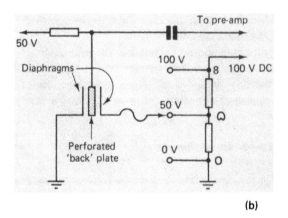

(b)

Figure 7.22 A variable polar diagram microphone (a) and simplified circuit (b).

One diaphragm (we'll think of it as the front one) is earthed. The back plate is at a potential which we'll take to be 50 V, while the potential of the rear diaphragm can be varied.

If the rear diaphragm is at 50 V it is at the same potential as the back plate, so the rear cardioid is ineffective, leaving only the front portion working.

If the rear diaphragm is at 0 V then the front and rear cardioids are both operative and working in the same phase. This means their polar diagrams are added together and if two cardioids are added the result is an omnidirectional pattern. The left cardioid can be represented by $r = 1 + \cos \theta$, the right one by $r = 1 - \cos \theta$. Add these and we get 2, a constant.

Giving the rear cardioid a potential of 100 V is equivalent to reversing its phase, so now we subtract instead of adding. It should be fairly easy to see that this results in a figure-of-eight characteristic.

Other polar diagrams, hypercardioid for instance, can be produced using intermediate potentials.

Many variable polar diagram microphones have a small switch on the body of the microphone itself, but on some models the switching is on a separate unit.

Pressure zone microphones

These are simply small, high quality omnidirectional units, often electrostatic capsules, mounted close to a surface. In some cases this surface is a metal plate 15–20 cm square. In others the microphone is fitted into, say, a circular piece of wood. The latter arrangement is useful for discussions where satisfactory recordings can be made if the participants are gathered around the microphone, which can be on the floor. In television work the microphone may be fixed to large sheets of clear Perspex.

It is sometimes claimed that the polar diagram of a pressure zone microphone is a hemisphere, but whether it is or not depends on where it is mounted. The relatively small metal plates mentioned above are far too small to give a hemispherical pattern except at high frequencies.

Radio microphones

There is space here for only the briefest outline of radio microphones. The reader can find out much more by studying the literature provided by manufacturers. Figure 7.23 is a photograph of a typical high quality radio microphone. This is intended to be used with the transmitter carried in a pocket or concealed somehow in the clothing. The transmitter contains batteries which will power it for at least 3 hours. A limiter (see later) is incorporated to prevent distortion if the sound levels at the microphone are too high. Usually the microphone is of the 'personal' type, but given the right connectors almost any kind of microphone can be used.

The receiver can be put in a convenient position and its output may be fed into a studio microphone socket, for example. The range can be anything from a few metres, at worst, to perhaps 50 m at best (200–400 m is just achievable in good conditions out of doors, but this shouldn't be relied upon). One factor which can reduce the working range is interference caused by reflections of the radio signals. The metalwork inside, say, a television studio can result in two paths

(a)

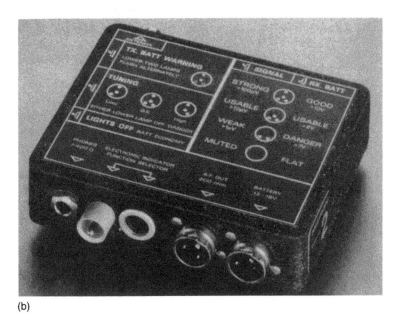

(b)

Figure 7.23 Radio microphone: (a) transmitter; (b) receiver

from transmitter to receiver. One is the direct path, the other is via reflection. If the two signals arrive at the receiver in phase then all is well, but if they are of comparable amplitudes and out of phase then cancellation occurs. There are systems known as *diversity reception* which have two or more receiving aerials and the system automatically selects the stronger signal.

Microphone sensitivities

There are several ways of indicating the sensitivity of a microphone, in other words the output that results from a given sound pressure level at the diaphragm. In some cases the output voltage for a standard pressure may be quoted. In others the output in decibels below a reference of 1 volt is given.

Table 7.1 sets out three commonly used sets of units. As a very rough guide a normal speaking voice at a distance of about half a metre produces a sound pressure level of the order of $1 N/m^2$.

Table 7.1 Microphone sensitivity

dB *relative to* $1 V/N/m^2 = 1 V/Pa$	mV/μbar	mV/10μbar	*Comments*
−20	9.5	95	Typical electrostatic microphones
−25	5.5	55	
−30	3.0	30	
−35	1.8	18	
−40	1.0	10	
−45	0.55	5.5	
−50	0.30	3.0	Typical moving-coil microphones
−55	0.18	1.8	
−60	0.10	1.0	Some ribbon microphones
−65	0.055	0.55	

8 Phantom power

Phantom power is simply a method of supplying microphones which need external power – electrostatic microphones – using conventional microphone plugs and sockets. Early electrostatic microphones used valves for their pre-amplifiers and this meant supplying the microphone with a low voltage (6 V) for the valve heater and a high voltage (100 V or more) for the valve anode. With the need for programme signal wires as well there had to be multi-core connectors and appropriate plugs and sockets for electrostatic microphones, whereas other non-powered microphones could have standard three-core cables with three-pin plugs and sockets. The usual procedure was to have the electrostatic microphones' power units on the studio floor, connected to suitable mains outlets, and the audio output went from the power unit to microphone sockets on the wall. All this complicated the rigging, required yet more cables on the studio floor and was expensive.

With the advent of suitable transistor devices for microphone pre-amplifiers it became possible to use a three-core cable for the power going in one direction and the audio signal going in the other. The term phantom power probably originated from a system of using two pairs of wires to carry three sets of signals in telephony. Because the third circuit had no separate physical existence it was called a phantom circuit.

There are two general methods of providing phantom power, as follows.

'Standard phantom', '48 V phantom'

Both these terms may be encountered and are usually taken to mean the same thing. The arrangement is shown in Figure 8.1. Forty-eight volts has been adopted more or less universally for this system. The power supplier's 48 V+ output is 'shared' between the programme wires. There are various ways in which this can be done; it could go to the centre tap of a transformer winding, but a very common method is to use a pair of resistors as in the diagram. These are of equal value and around 5 kohm is typical. (Resistors are cheaper and less bulky than transformers. Also they limit the current in the event of a short circuit.)

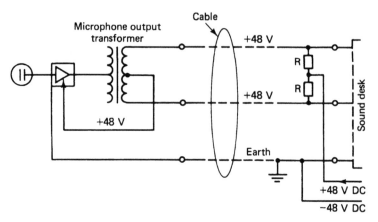

Figure 8.1 Standard phantom powering

The important thing to realize is that *there is no DC potential between the programme wires.*

At the microphone end the output transformer's centre tap is used to take the 48 V+ and feed it to the pre-amplifier, while the earth provides a return path for the 48 V−.

It should be clear that any non-power microphone – a moving coil, for example – could be plugged into the system and be quite unaware of the presence of the 48 V, provided of course that the microphone is itself 'balanced', which really means that it has an output transformer for the audio and a separate earth.

In recent years it has become normal for manufacturers of sound desks to incorporate phantom powering so that any electrostatic microphone which is plugged into the desk receives the power it needs. Some desks have switches on each channel to cut the 48 V if necessary.

'A-B powering', 'modulation lead powering'

This is illustrated in Figure 8.2 and is mostly used where only one microphone is to be fed from a battery which is remote from the microphone. The usual voltage is around 9–12 V, the latter being the specified standard, and, as the diagram shows, capacitors confine the DC to the actual cable. A typical use is to feed gun microphones used with film or electronic news gathering (ENG) equipment where a 48 V battery supply might be inconvenient.

An occasional problem with this type of powering is that a phase reversal in the cable, which might not matter in pure audio terms, causes an inversion of the supply with the result that the microphone doesn't work.

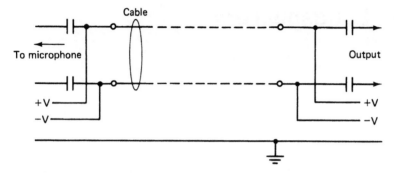

Cable

To microphone

Output

+V
−V

+V
−V

Figure 8.2 A-B (modulation lead powering)

Facts about phantom power

1. Where a manufacturer produces two versions of a microphone, one for 48 V working and the other for A-B working, additional characters are usually added to the type number. The interpretation may or may not be obvious. For example, the two versions of a particular microphone made by one company are MKH 816 P 48 U-3 and MKH 816 TU-3. The '48' in the first gives a reasonable clue to the fact that it uses 48 V phantom power, but only by referring to the manufacturer's data would one know that the second microphone used a 12 V A-B system.
2. There can be loud noises from monitoring loudspeakers if microphones are plugged into a phantom-powered system when faders are open (i.e. faded up).
3. Having all the studio microphones which need power deriving that power from a single source may seem to be asking for trouble. In fact the reliability of phantom power systems is good and in any case it is quite usual to have a second back-up power supply with automatic changeover in the event of a failure.

9 Loudspeakers

Just as with a microphone, there are three basic components of a loudspeaker:

1. A radiating surface (the equivalent of a microphone's diaphragm).
2. The transducer. Here the job of the transducer is to convert electrical energy into mechanical movement, and not the other way round, as in a microphone, although small loudspeakers are sometimes made to work as microphones.
3. The enclosure or cabinet.

The radiating surface

Assuming that a lot of sound has to be produced, the radiating surface has to set a correspondingly large amount of air into vibration. This means a big area for the surface and/or a large to-and-fro movement. Usually a big area is the easier option as there can be very definite restrictions on the distortionless movement that a practical transducer can provide.

The ideal surface would be a rigid piston. If this existed then the air particle movements in front of it would all be in phase. It is possible to make a rigid piston which will vibrate satisfactorily at low frequencies, but at higher frequencies a reasonably-sized piston made of any known material will flex, as in Figure 9.1, unless it is so massive that a quite impossible amount of power would be needed to drive it.

There have been many attempts to make rigid pistons for loudspeakers but they have been largely unsuccessful for one reason or another. (The electrostatic loudspeaker – see later – goes a long way towards overcoming this problem, but not by having a rigid material as the radiating surface. Instead it is made to move uniformly by driving it over its entire area.) What *has* been successful is the cone-shaped radiator. A little thought will show that at high frequencies the air particles in front will not all be moving in the same phase, because they originate from different points along the axis. However, if the cone angle is large, and different cones are used for different frequencies, then any phase effects caused by the cone shape are generally negligible.

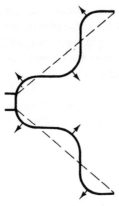

Figure 9.1 Movements of a 'rigid' piston

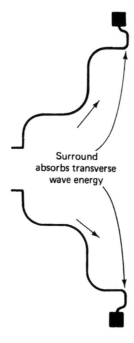

Surround
absorbs transverse
wave energy

Figure 9.2 The cone surround

Cone materials

A form of fibrous paper-like substance which can be moulded while it is wet has been a popular material for many years and is still used in low-cost units. For high-grade work it has been found to be less than ideal because the fibres in it, although apparently random, may nevertheless show localized tendencies to have a measure of alignment. This can cause slightly anomalous properties in the cone behaviour. A favoured substance in many monitoring loudspeakers is *polypropylene*, a plastic which can be given the correct shape by drawing it down over a mould by a vacuum when the plastic is hot.

The *cone surround* (Figure 9.2) is important. It needs to absorb wave energy travelling along the cone from the centre. If this isn't done then the wave energy may be reflected with the result that standing waves are set up.

The transducer

Many systems could in principle be used to convert electrical power into movement, but only a few are really satisfactory in practice. Some work well over a limited frequency range and we will deal with those later.

Electrostatic loudspeaker

This has a large sheet of a material such as aluminium, or possibly an alloy of it, positioned between two metal grids to form the radiating surface. A large DC voltage is applied between the metal sheet and the grids and the audio signal is superimposed upon the DC. The varying electrostatic force causes the sheet to vibrate and produce sound waves. The reason for having the vibrating sheet between the grids is to reduce distortion. If only one grid were used the force, which is proportional to $1/(\text{distance})^2$, would have a significantly non-linear characteristic. A change in the applied signal voltage of, say, 10 V would have a greater effect when the sheet was close to the grid than when it was farther from it. Two grids cause this effect to be greatly reduced because, to put it simply, as the sheet moves away from one grid it moves nearer the other and the distortion is effectively 'cancelled out'.

Electrostatic loudspeakers can be capable of very good quality reproduction, especially as they are free from the spurious frequencies known as *colorations*. The drawbacks are that high sound levels are difficult to produce, the extreme bass frequencies tend to be weak, and the device has a figure-of-eight sound radiation pattern. This can result in troublesome effects from the back radiation. Because of these the electrostatic loudspeaker has not found favour in professional circles, although owners of them in domestic set-ups often regard all other kinds of loudspeaker as poor substitutes!

Moving-coil unit

Figure 9.3 shows the principle of this unit. The similarity to the transducer in a moving-coil microphone is obvious, but in practice there are important

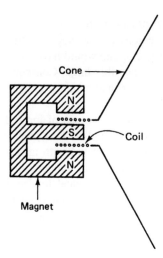

Figure 9.3 Moving-coil loudspeaker transducer

differences. Here space allows only a brief mention of two of these – for more detail the reader should look at a book dealing only with loudspeakers.

To begin with the coil often has to dissipate a fair amount of heat. A moderate-sized monitoring loudspeaker may easily be handling 50 watts of power at times – a large public address loudspeaker may be handling many times more. In the latter cooling fans may be used to remove the heat, but quiet though they may be fans are too noisy for studio monitoring conditions.

Also it is essential that the coil movement is never so great that it results in any non-linearity – that is, coil movement must always be proportional to the current flowing in it – otherwise there is distortion.

Other transducer systems

The electrostatic transducer and the moving-coil unit are all basically microphones 'working backwards'. Two other systems follow this idea. One makes use of the piezo-electric effect, in which a suitable slice of a crystal deforms slightly when a voltage is applied (compare with the crystal microphone). The movement is very small and any radiating surface attached to it cannot easily produce low frequencies, where air particle movements are much greater than at high frequencies. High-frequency operation only is therefore practicable – hence the *piezo-electric tweeter*. ('Tweeter', originally a slang term which has now become respectable, means a loudspeaker which handles high frequencies only.)

Other tweeters have used the ribbon principle, very much like a ribbon microphone but with power supplied to the ribbon. Again, low-frequency power handling is the problem. A practical ribbon cannot move great distances without going outside the linear regions of the magnetic flux. A large ribbon is quite unrealistic because the magnetic gap would have to be correspondingly big, and then the magnet would be impossibly large. Consequently *ribbon tweeters* have found favour with some designers and manufacturers, but they are of little use for general loudspeaker applications.

A final mention can be made of the use of ionized air. If a radio frequency signal of high enough voltage is applied to a pair of electrodes in air then a discharge occurs. If the RF is modulated with an audio signal the ionized air undergoes corresponding fluctuations in temperature, so that sound waves are produced. In theory this is almost the ideal loudspeaker because there are no mechanical moving parts – other than the air molecules. Size restrictions have meant that the principle has been limited, again, to tweeters.

The moving-coil drive unit has been found, despite difficulties and imperfections, to be the most generally satisfactory transducer for most purposes. It is reliable and any one unit can handle a reasonably wide frequency range. Indeed, if the unit is not too large, perhaps 20 cm or so in diameter, and high output powers are not essential, it is possible to deal with a frequency range from around 100 Hz to 12 kHz – not enough for real quality reproduction but possibly more than adequate for many applications. We shall see later how a full audio range is covered using two or more units.

The enclosure

The box or cabinet in which the drive unit(s) are mounted is much more important than might appear at first sight. The reason for this is that there is a major problem caused by sound radiation from the rear of the cone. To begin with, if the cone moves forward it creates a compression in front and a rarefaction behind, so that the rear radiation is *out of phase* with the front radiation. Imagine an isolated cone unit as in Figure 9.4.

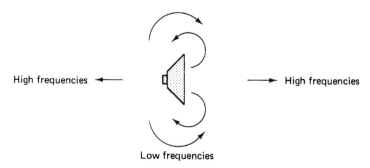

High frequencies ←———   ———→ High frequencies

Low frequencies

Figure 9.4 Unmounted cone

The lower frequency sounds, whose wavelength is greater than the cone diameter, will bend round by diffraction, those from the front going to the rear and those from the rear bending round to the front. Since the rear radiation is in anti-phase with the front radiation this means that there is marked cancellation. The high frequencies can be assumed to do little bending because of their relatively short wavelength, and will then move in more or less straight beams. The net result is that there is little low-frequency sound produced. Figure 9.5 shows the likely frequency response curve for a 25 cm diameter cone.

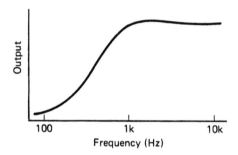

Figure 9.5 Frequency response graph for an unmounted 25 cm cone (simplified)

The answer to this poor response is to get rid of the radiation from the rear of the cone. But how? There are three possible answers, of which one is to pretend that there isn't too much of a problem. This is the one adopted by manufacturers of some television sets and low-cost radios. The two remaining answers are:

1. Try to absorb the rear radiation.
2. Manipulate it so that it is actually useful.

The first of these brings us to:

The sealed enclosure

Basically this is simply a well-made (as rigid as possible) box containing sound-absorbing materials and sealed to prevent the leakage of sound waves (Figure 9.6). This arrangement can work quite well but it doesn't give a completely satisfactory answer. The reason is that at low frequencies the cone movement, as we have said, has to be relatively large. With a sealed enclosure, unless it is very big, the cone has difficulty in compressing the air in the box when it moves back, and rarefying the air when it moves forward. This springiness of the air modifies the performance of the cone and drive unit, raising the lowest frequency at which

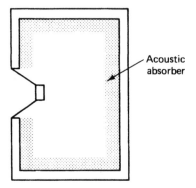

Figure 9.6 Sealed loudspeaker enclosure

it is effective. To put that another way, suppose the cone/coil assembly could vibrate perfectly well down to, say, 30 Hz when it is unmounted; in the enclosure this lower limit may well be more like 60 Hz, or possibly higher.

Facts about sealed enclosure loudspeakers

1. The limited bass response means that they are not really suitable for serious monitoring purposes (but see Fact 4 below).
2. However, the effect of 'false bass' (see Chapter 4) can make them sound better than perhaps they are.
3. Very acceptable loudspeakers having sealed enclosures can be made with overall volumes no greater than $0.01 \, m^3$ – say 30 cm high by 18 cm by 15 cm.
4. These small sizes mean that sealed enclosure speakers can be used in professional environments where space is limited and the compromise which trades quality for size is acceptable.
5. The small size means that very high sound levels cannot be produced.
6. Because the sealed enclosure is equivalent, theoretically, to mounting the unit on an infinitely large board ('baffle') to prevent the rear radiation getting round to the front, this type of unit is sometimes called an *infinite baffle* loudspeaker.

Some loudspeaker designers have used a labyrinth inside the enclosure to help absorb the rear radiation. These have tended to be somewhat larger than the sealed enclosure we have described.

The vented enclosure

Earlier we said that one way of dealing with the cone's rear radiation was to manipulate it so that it was useful. This is done, partially, in the *vented enclosure*

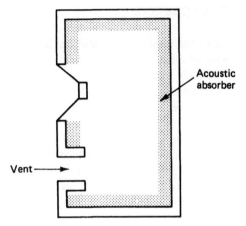

Figure 9.7 Vented loudspeaker

(sometimes called the *bass reflex* cabinet). Remember that the high frequencies are not too serious a problem. Those from the front move out and keep going. Those at the rear can be fairly easily absorbed. The low frequencies, on the other hand, bend round the cone if they can and also, having long wavelengths, they are less easy to absorb without inconvenient thicknesses of absorber. The trick is to make the whole of the enclosure into a Helmholtz resonator (see Chapter 6). This is done by making a vent somewhere, usually at the front of the cabinet, and letting the rest of the inside of the cabinet be the body of the resonator (Figure 9.7).

The resonator is usually tuned to around 30 Hz, to boost the response where it would otherwise be falling off. The interesting thing is that now the air movements in the vent are *in phase with the front radiation from the cone!* With care a response down to 30 Hz, or even perhaps lower, can be produced.

Facts about vented enclosure loudspeakers

1. They have to be fairly large. Around 0.1 m³ is a practical minimum. In linear terms this could be 50 cm high, 45 cm wide and 40 cm deep. Most are very much bigger than this.
2. The vent can be no more than a hole, usually circular, in the cabinet, the thickness of the cabinet material providing the length of the vent.
3. The *damping*, i.e. the amount of friction controlling the resonance, is important. If there is too much damping then the resonator does not produce enough low-frequency output. If there is too little damping then there may be an undesirable peak at the resonant frequency.
4. High-grade monitoring loudspeakers almost invariably have vented enclosures.

Multiple unit loudspeakers

It should be fairly clear from what we have said that it is virtually impossible to achieve a high sound-level output *and* a wide frequency response from a single unit. To be capable of high sound levels the cone has to be large; it is then relatively heavy (strictly speaking we should say it has a relatively large *mass*), and this means that the cone cannot be made to vibrate easily at the higher frequencies.

The obvious answer is to have more than one drive unit, each one designed to handle a specific frequency band. Many such loudspeakers have three units: a bass unit ('woofer'), a mid-range unit (occasionally called the 'squawker') and a high-frequency unit, which we have already mentioned, called a 'tweeter'. Figure 9.8 illustrates the idea.

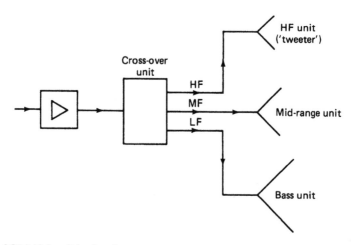

Figure 9.8 Multiple unit loudspeaker

The *cross-over* units are frequency-dividing circuits that ensure that each drive unit is fed only with its correct frequency band. Designing cross-over units is difficult:

1. The transition from one frequency band to the next must be smooth – the overlap must be such that the overall response does not have dips or peaks at these regions.
2. The fact that considerable power may be fed to the drive units means that the components in the cross-over units must be capable of handling relatively large currents without overheating. In fact it has been found that with some loudspeakers the overall response is different when producing high sound

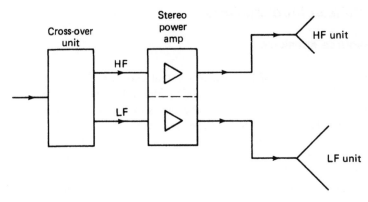

Figure 9.9 Low-level cross-over units

levels compared with low levels. Variations in component values, caused by heating, have resulted in changes in the cross-over's response.

Because of these problems the cost of good cross-over units has sometimes been very high. An interesting solution has been to use *low-level* cross-overs. In other words the power amplifiers come *after* and not before the cross-over units (Figure 9.9).

With this particular design it has been found possible to cover the frequency range from 30 Hz to about 16 kHz using only two drive units. This means that a commercial stereo power amplifier can be used, one half feeding the low-frequency unit, the other half feeding the tweeter. (A stereo power amplifier costs less than two separate mono amplifiers having otherwise similar characteristics.)

Facts about loudspeakers

1. Their efficiency is low. A high-quality loudspeaker may have an efficiency of as little as 1–2%. For example, 50 W of *electrical* power fed into such a loudspeaker may result in as little as 0.5 W of *acoustic* power.
2. The positioning of speakers can be very critical. Most should be a specified distance, often around half a metre, above the floor. The bass output is likely to be reduced if the speaker is positioned much above the recommended height. Also they should not normally be placed too close to corners of a room.
3. Because of diffraction effects the high frequencies tend to be concentrated on the axis of the speaker. Careful design can give a reasonable spread, but for quality listening a position on the axis is to be preferred.
4. Good quality monitoring loudspeakers should be capable of producing sound levels of 115 dBA at a distance of one metre.

Specialized loudspeakers

Line-source speakers

An important category of loudspeakers is that known as *line-source* or *column* speakers. These are widely used in public address (PA) applications and will be referred to later under that heading. The aim is to produce a loudspeaker which is directional. This is important in PA because, as we shall see, it is generally vital that as little loudspeaker sound as possible finds its way back into the microphones. The ideal would be to have a loudspeaker whose radiation pattern could be varied (rather like a variable polar diagram microphone) and could range from a narrow beam to thin slices of sound, either vertically or horizontally. A fortune awaits the designer of a compact and low-cost device having this characteristic! Unfortunately the laws of physics make it unlikely that anyone will ever produce such a unit. However, loudspeakers with a degree of directional radiation are indeed possible.

Figure 9.10 shows a system of several separate drive units mounted one above the other in a suitable enclosure. They form a *line* of sound *sources*, or they could be thought of as being in a *column* – hence the two names.

It should be fairly obvious that on the axis of the system the sound waves from all the units are in phase and will therefore reinforce each other. Off this axis the different path lengths from the units will tend to cause cancellation, so that there is, in general, a reduction in the sound level. However, a moment's thought will show that phase cancellation can only occur if the wavelengths are comparable

Figure 9.10 Basic line source loudspeaker

with, or less than, the length of the loudspeaker column. For example, a column two metres high will have little directional properties below about 150 Hz.

In the horizontal plane, assuming the column is vertical, the radiation will be much as it would be from a conventional loudspeaker having the same cross section – in other words fairly omnidirectional except at high frequencies. Figure 9.11 shows the sort of radiation patterns to be expected from a line-source loudspeaker.

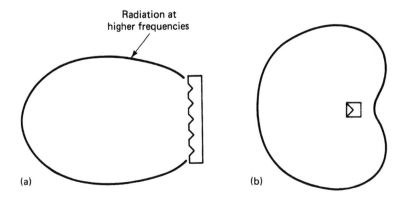

Figure 9.11 Radiation from a line-source loudspeaker: (a) vertically; (b) horizontally

Facts about line-source loudspeakers

1. The quality of reproduction is generally well below that of monitoring loudspeakers. It is often speech quality only, but to be fair that is usually all that is needed.
2. Good quality units do exist but they tend to be both large and expensive.
3. To reduce the problems which can arise in a PA situation from the more or less omnidirectional characteristic at low frequencies the bass response is frequently 'rolled-off' below about 160 Hz.

Horn loudspeakers

These will be mentioned only briefly as their use in the professional broadcasting and recording world is generally small. A trumpet-shaped horn which opens out in an *exponential* (i.e. logarithmic) manner provides a very good way of matching the acoustic characteristics of a small drive unit to the air. The most common use of such loudspeakers is for outdoor public address at, say, race courses. The quality in these situations is usually poor – 'tinny' is about the right description. However, very good quality can be produced provided that:

1. The horn is large. This means a diameter at the open end of a couple of metres or more.
2. The 'flare' is not too rapid. A length of at least seven or eight metres is desirable.
3. The material of the horn does not vibrate itself. Rigid materials are thus necessary. (Some have been constructed out of concrete.)

The three provisos above are enough to show why horn loudspeakers are not widely used in studios! One interesting feature of horn units is that they can be very efficient. Figures of around 20% efficiency are claimed – compare this with the 1–2% of a conventional loudspeaker. The above comments apply to horn loudspeakers intended to cover the entire, or almost the entire, audio range. Nevertheless there are a number of quality loudspeakers on the market which use horns to increase efficiency over a limited frequency range.

Loud-hailers generally have a 're-entrant' horn. Sections of a horn are, as it were, folded back so that the overall length is small. The metal construction makes these units weatherproof and the higher efficiency is a bonus with battery-driven apparatus.

Listening tests

The only way to compare loudspeakers is by listening tests. Assuming two or more loudspeakers are all of fairly good quality it is quite impossible to evaluate them except by direct and immediate comparison of their outputs. One very important reason for this is that the ear's memory for *accurate* recall lasts only for one or two seconds. It is quite impossible to listen to one good loudspeaker on Monday, listen to another good one on Friday and then say that which was better of the two. (If they are very different so that one is good and the other is mediocre then such statements may be valid.)

Comparison of graphs and other measurements is not, in practice, usually very helpful. *Transient responses* are not shown up at all well in measurements. Also let us not forget that the ear is a far more sensitive and accurate assessor of quality than any man-made instrument. Some fundamental rules for evaluation of the qualities of loudspeakers are:

1. Test only two loudspeakers at a time.
2. Place them side-by-side in as good a listening room as possible.
3. Don't rely on one person's judgement if other experienced ears are available.

4. Play a wide range of material over the loudspeakers – pop music, orchestral music, speech, and so on.
5. Use as clickless a switch as possible to cut from one unit to the other. Try to avoid switching at the ends of phrases or bars in the music. Changes in instrumentation may obscure small quality differences.
6. Don't be bamboozled. It is very easy to be misled by things like the appearance of the loudspeaker, what colleagues say about it, the music being played, and so on.

10 Basic stereo

How we locate sounds

The purpose of stereo (in full, 'stereophony') is to create for a listener the illusion that there is spread of sounds between a pair of loudspeakers and that this image is an accurate, or at least a plausible, representation of the spread of sounds in front of the microphones. To see how this can happen requires an understanding of how we locate sounds normally.

Several processes are involved in *binaural hearing*. The most important is the *time-of-arrival difference* at the ears, as shown in Figure 10.1. Here, sounds

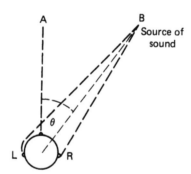

Figure 10.1 Time-of-arrival difference

arriving from A – straight in front of the listener – enter both ears at the same instant. Sounds from B, though, enter the right ear earlier than they enter the left ear, creating a *time-of-arrival difference*. The brain can use this time difference to estimate the angle which is represented in the diagram by θ. This is apparently because from early childhood we learn to associate certain angles with particular time-of-arrival differences. What is almost incredible is the smallness of some of these differences. Imagine a sound arriving from the extreme right. The path difference between the right and left ears, for the average human, is in the region of 30 cm. This corresponds to a time difference of about 1 ms. At the other end of the range it is generally true that most people can detect a movement of a sound source when it moves from the centre line through about 1° of arc. A simple calculation shows that the time-of-arrival difference is then rather less than 10 μs!

Other factors are, as we've said, involved in the location of sounds. These include:

1. *Sound wave amplitude differences at the two ears*. At low frequencies diffraction effects mean that the amplitudes at both ears will be the same. At higher frequencies – some authorities quote 700 Hz and above – there will be some amplitude differences and these can help the brain to assess sound directions.
2. *Common sense*. The sound of a blackbird heard from inside one's sitting room is probably coming from the direction of a window.
3. *Visual clues*. If we hear music in a room and we can see a loudspeaker then it's very likely that we shall assume the music comes out of the loudspeaker. But beware! It is possible to be very misled. Sometimes strong visual clues can lead to quite the wrong conclusion about the source of a sound.

Steady tones are difficult or even impossible to locate. There needs to be some form of relatively low frequency modulation to give the brain a chance to compare arrival times at the ears.

If we now think about sound reproduction from two loudspeakers it's fairly obvious that visual clues cannot be used. (Stereo television might seem to be an exception but even the larger screens at present available for home use are unlikely to give much of a visual clue to the apparent source of a sound.) Item 2, common sense, is difficult to assess as a factor, but on its own it can't be much use in stereo reproduction. Amplitude differences at the two ears may not be very significant when the loudspeakers are in fixed positions. So we are left with time-of-arrival differences. Therefore any practical stereo system must simulate time-of-arrival differences. Next we'll see how this can be done.

Creating artificial time-of-arrival differences

Figure 10.2 represents two loudspeakers with a listener on the centre line between them. Let us suppose that the sound from the left-hand speaker is very much larger in amplitude than that from the right. We will use here the convention of denoting stereo left by A and right by B. (The alphabet when written has A on the left and B on the right!)

The next thing is to see what happens at the listener's ears. This is illustrated in Figure 10.3. In (a) we are seeing what happens at the listener's *left* ear. The large amplitude sound from loudspeaker A arrives first, the smaller signal from B arrives a little later roughly ⅓ ms later if the listener and the loudspeakers form

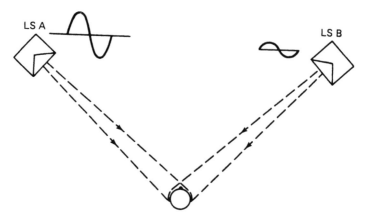

Figure 10.2 Different amplitude sounds from a pair of loudspeakers

an equilateral triangle. The sound wave that strikes the left eardrum is the *sum* of these two waves, shown in (b). Now the *right* ear (c). The weaker sound from loudspeaker B arrives first, the larger one from A later, and their sum (d) is what affects the right eardrum. Now if we compare carefully the addition wave in (b) with the addition wave in (d) we see that the wave in (b) is slightly in advance of the wave in (d). In other words we have in effect a time-of-arrival difference. Notice that if sounds arrive at the listener from the front there will be a symmetry that results in the addition waves occurring at the same time – so no time-of-arrival difference.

The lesson is quite clear, even if at first sight paradoxical. To simulate *time-of-arrival differences* at the listener's ears we must have *amplitude differences* between the A and B signals. We shall see shortly how amplitude differences in the A and B signals can be created.

Phase of stereo signals

In thinking about amplitude differences we must also take into account their *phase*. Phase is very important in stereo. What it means is that the A and B signals must be in phase although they will in general be of differing amplitudes. If the signals are out of phase, and this can result from incorrectly wired equipment for example, the listener's brain is being given something that is outside normal experience. In real life it is virtually impossible to have totally out-of-phase sounds arriving at the ears, at least for anything other than a very brief moment. Consequently out-of-phase stereo causes confusion in the brain. It is then very difficult to locate the image – it may seem behind, or inside the head, but when one turns the image moves to somewhere else. The effect is generally

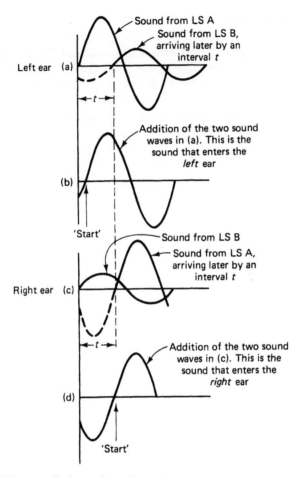

Figure 10.3 Different amplitude sounds at a listener's ears

rather unpleasant and can induce headaches if experienced for any length of time. There have even been reports of physical nausea. We shall refer to phase again later.

Production of stereo signals

Basically there are two ways of producing stereo signals:

1. Using a pair of microphones.
2. Using a single microphone and electrically splitting its output into two normally unequal parts.

Pairs of microphones

First we must introduce an item of terminology – *channel*. This means, in a stereo context, a path for one of the two signals. Thus the A channel is the electrical route for the left-hand signals from microphone right through to loudspeaker.

Figure 10.4 shows a pair of microphones with their diaphragms very close together. They are shown as cardioids, but that is just for convenience. The actual polar diagram doesn't matter much, so long as the two microphones are not omnidirectional. What is important is that the two polar diagrams are as closely matched as possible. The A microphone is connected to the A channel, the B microphone to the B channel and the angle between them is shown as being about 90°, but in practice there may be some latitude about this.

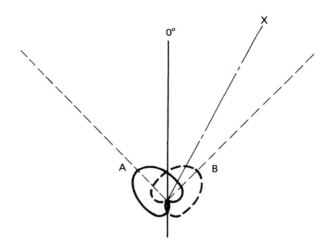

Figure 10.4 A pair of closely mounted microphones

Suppose sound approaches from the front, from the 0° direction. The resulting signals in the A and B channels will be the same. This means that there will be no apparent time-of-arrival difference at the listener's ears.

If sound arrives from X then there will be a larger amplitude signal in the B channel than in the A and this, as we have seen, will give the listener the impression that the sound image is somewhere to the right of the centre line.

So a pair of closely-spaced microphones meets the requirements for producing stereo signals. We shall see later what happens if the microphones are not closely spaced, or if they are not cardioids.

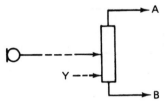

Figure 10.5 A potential divider system

Electrical methods

Figure 10.5 shows a single microphone whose output is fed into a potential divider. This is a simplified diagram, amplifiers and other items of equipment having been omitted in the interests of simplicity. The potential divider is called a *panpot*, or *pan*oramic *pot*ential divider. Clearly, if the slider is in the centre of its travel the microphone's output is split equally between the A and B channels. But if it is nearer one end than the other, at Y say, then the signal in the B channel will be greater than in the A channel and we have the required amplitude difference.

Notice that in neither of the two systems we have just looked at are any time differences introduced – purely amplitude differences between the two channels.

Both systems have their applications and we will look at these later. First we will study the microphone pair arrangement in more detail.

Coincident pair arrangements

A pair of closely-spaced microphones is known as a *coincident pair*. It is the *diaphragms* which need to be closely spaced, so that they are, as far as possible, coincident in space.

Given information about the angle between the microphones and their polar diagram it is possible to predict reasonably well what the stereo sound imaging will be. However, we need to have some data relating the all-important amplitude differences with positions of apparent stereo images, and this is shown in Figure 10.6. Here, the vertical axis shows *interchannel difference* (ICD). This is simply the ratio of one channel amplitude to the other channel amplitude expressed in decibels. The horizontal axis gives the probable image position, C is central between the loudspeakers and R/L implies that the sound image is at either the right or the left loudspeaker. The graph is approximate, as different people interpret interchannel differences in slightly different ways. Also, and this is very curious, if the signals to the loudspeakers are interchanged the graph for any one person is apt to be different. To put that another way, for signals giving images

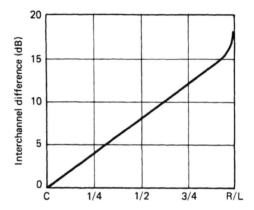

Figure 10.6 Interchannel differences against image position

from centre to right the graph is slightly different from one giving images from centre to left – almost as if there were some sort of 'left-handedness'.

Although Figure 10.6 is approximate it is nevertheless good enough for our purposes. To begin with, we can see that if one channel amplitude is greater than the other by some 18 dB or more the sound image is shifted into that channel's loudspeaker.

Also for every 6 dB increase in ICD the image moves very roughly one-third of the distance from centre to edge. The reason for picking on this particular approximation is that *6 dB represents a doubling of any voltage involved*. Now let's take another look at a pair of cardioid microphones arranged as a coincident pair.

In Figure 10.7 it's clear that sounds arriving from W, on the axis of the pair, will produce the same output signal in each microphone. We've already seen

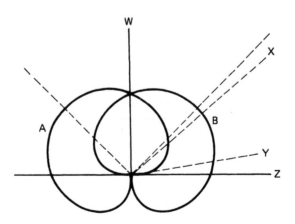

Figure 10.7 Interchannel differences from two microphones

that this will result in an apparently central image for the centrally placed listener.

Look now at sounds arriving from X. For this particular angle the output of the right-facing (B) microphone will be twice the output of the A microphone. B's output is then 6 dB higher, and going by the approximation above this means that the sound image will be about one-third of the way from centre to right. Similarly, sounds coming from the direction of Y will produce about four times the output from B than from A. This represents 12 dB and the sound image will be about two-thirds of the way from left to right. And for sounds arriving from Z there is no significant output from A, the interchannel differences will be at least 18 dB, and the sound image will be at the right-hand loudspeaker.

Obviously the image positions deduced in this way are only approximate, but they give a very reasonable guide in practice. Anyway the situation is apt to be complicated by the acoustics of the listening room and by the fact that different people may perceive different locations for the same interchannel difference. The point is that, given the polar diagrams of the microphone pair, it is possible to predict with quite adequate accuracy the resulting spread of stereo images.

Here it will be enough to summarize the main results. We will use the term *angle of acceptance* to mean the total sound source angle at the microphones to give a full, loudspeaker-to-loudspeaker, stereo image. Figure 10.8 illustrates this.

A figure-of-eight pair needs a few extra comments. As Figure 10.9 shows, there is a 90° angle of acceptance at both the front and back of the pair. Also the side quadrants can cause problems because they are out-of-phase regions. This is because the two lobes of a figure-of-eight microphone should be thought of as

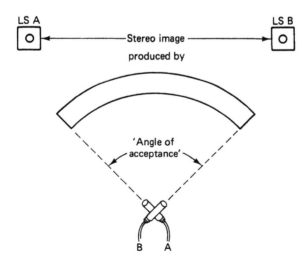

Figure 10.8 'Angle of acceptance'

Table 10.1 Approximate angles of acceptance for microphones at 90°

Polar diagram	Angle of acceptance
Figure-of-eight	90° at front with another 90° lobe at rear
Hypercardioid	130–140°
Cardioid	180°

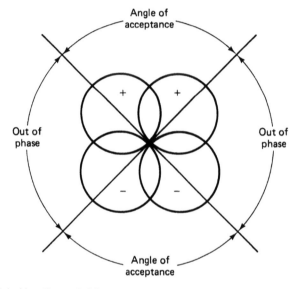

Figure 10.9 Coincident figure-of-eights

having opposite polarities. (Suppose a particular frontal sound causes the diaphragm to move inwards at the start of the sound. Exactly the same sound from the rear will cause an opposite diaphragm movement.) Thus at the sides of the pair a sound source will be picked up on the front lobe of one microphone and the rear lobe of the other – it will be out of phase, totally out of phase at 90° and 270° and partially out of phase at the other angles of the side quadrants. We've already seen that out-of-phase conditions are to be avoided, so the side quadrants have to be regarded as 'forbidden' regions. Sound sources in these directions will be difficult to locate. Reverberation, however, can be picked up in the out-of-phase angles without generally being unpleasant to the listener – it is too diffuse to have any definite phase characteristics. Similarly, it is sometimes possible for applause to be acceptable.

Coincident pairs and panpots – applications

Earlier we said that basically there are two ways of using microphones for stereo sound pick-up. One we have just dealt with – coincident pairs – the other was mentioned briefly and illustrated in Figure 10.6. We need to say very little more about it here, except that the actual design of a panpot may be rather more complicated than Figure 10.5 shows. However, it may be worthwhile to indicate something of the applications of the two microphone systems. We shall not go into detail as that would not be appropriate to this book. In brief:

● coincident pairs can be used when the sound sources in front of the microphone are at least reasonably *internally balanced* – that is, the relative loudness of the various parts of the band or orchestra are controlled by the leader or conductor. An audience sitting in the studio would hear an acceptable version of the music.
● Mono microphones and panpots are necessary when there is no internal balance in the band. Much light and pop music falls into this category. The balance of the instruments is achieved by a 'balancer' sitting at a sound control desk. A coincident pair used in such a studio would produce a quite unacceptable sound output.

In practice it is quite usual to see mono microphones being used to reinforce sections of, say, a symphony orchestra even though a coincident pair is doing most of the work. (Sometimes more than one coincident pair may be used, one pair covering perhaps a choir, the other covering the orchestra.)

Coincident pairs are also almost the only way of covering radio drama. At the same time it must be added that it is not unusual to cover things like symphony orchestras with mono microphones and panpots. It is largely a matter of taste.

Spaced microphones

It's quite obvious that, despite the term 'coincident pair' microphones, no two things can be truly coincident in space. There must be some distance between the diaphragms. This leads to the question of how close the microphones must be in practice. Can they be separated by an appreciable distance? Briefly, the answer is yes, up to a point.

We've already established the rule that the A and B channels must differ only in amplitude. Suppose, now, that we have two microphones spaced 4–5 m apart as in Figure 10.10.

It should be clear that there will indeed be amplitude differences in the A and B channels, but there will also be time differences. What is likely to happen for the listener is that his or her ears and brain will make use of the amplitude difference to create an effective time-of-arrival difference, as we've seen, but the

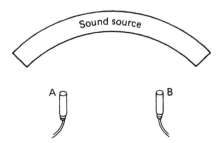

Figure 10.10 Widely spaced microphones

time differences in the two channels will also be perceived. In other words there will be too much time-of-arrival effect – the stereo image will be greatly exaggerated and the probable result is that the images will be on the extreme left and extreme right only, with little or no central images. This gives what is known as a *hole in the middle*. (Many early stereo recordings from around the late 1950s show this admirably!)

As the microphones are brought closer together the hole in the middle gets less obvious, and may not be at all apparent when the separation is less than a metre or so. Many commercial recordings are made in this way; quite often with a third microphone between the other two but above them. The drawback is that *compatibility*, a subject we will deal with next, is apt to suffer. Also many people consider that the accuracy of the stereo images is less good with microphones spaced even a few centimetres apart.

Compatibility: the M and S signals

In any broadcast situation it will normally be assumed that while the listeners/ viewers with stereo equipment are the main target there are nevertheless large numbers of people listening in mono. The problem is to make sure that there is reasonable *compatibility* – that is, the mono listeners will obviously not receive the directional effects but they should not lose out in other respects. In particular the relative balance of parts of the sound image may change in going from stereo to mono. To see how this can happen we must first look at variants of the A and B signals.

It is standard practice to refer to the addition of the A and B signals as the *M signal*. Thus:

$$A + B = M$$

Also the difference between A and B is the *S signal*:

$$A - B = S$$

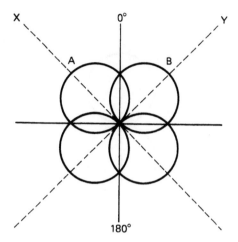

Figure 10.11 Coincident figure-of-eights

or B − A = S, depending on which is greater, A or B. We shall write A − B = S, regardless of which of the two is the greater.

The M signal is the mono signal; a listener in mono will simply receive the addition of the two stereo signals. We shall see this in a different context when we look at stereo transmission systems. (Historically the M stood for *middle* – the central sound signals – and S for *side*. However, it may help to think of M as standing for the mono and S for the stereo or directional component.)

Now let us look again at a coincident pair microphone arrangement. This time we'll consider a pair of figure-of-eight microphones (Figure 10.11). To see what the M signal looks like involves adding the sensitivities of the two microphones at different angles – something the reader might care to do with a ruler having first drawn the four touching circles. The result is shown in Figure 10.12. It is a forward-facing figure-of-eight. Incidentally the S signal is also a figure-of-eight, but turned through 90°.

We can now begin to see where compatibility comes in. Imagine that there is a spread of sound sources ranging from X to Y across the front of the microphone pair in Figure 10.11. The stereo image will spread from the left to the right loudspeakers with, we can assume, more or less equal loudness. The mono listener will receive only the M signal, and this will be equivalent to a single figure-of-eight placed in the same position. Looking at Figure 10.12 we see that sound sources at X and Y will not be picked up as well as central sounds – they will appear quieter to the listener. There is thus likely to be a change in the sound balance in going from stereo to mono. Whether this is serious in practice depends on the nature of the programme, but a good sound balancer will check the compatibility from time to time by switching the monitoring loudspeakers from stereo to mono, and preferably mono on *one* loudspeaker only as this simulates

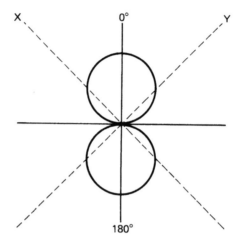

Figure 10.12 M signal for a pair of figure-of-eight microphones

better the listening conditions for the mono listener. (Mono on two loudspeakers sounds better than on one.)

Try sketching different polar diagrams for coincident pairs and verify, at least approximately, that the corresponding M signals are those given in Table 10.2. The last line may seem surprising, but back-to-back cardioids, as they are usually known, are favoured by some sound balancers. In theory the omnidirectional M signal gives perfect compatibility, but in practice things may not be quite that simple.

So far we've used coincident pair microphones to show how compatibility may be affected. We don't escape the problem by using mono microphones and panpots. Imagine a sound image has been panned fully left (say). There is then an A signal only. Now since

$$A + B = M$$

and

$$A - B = S$$

Adding these gives

$$A = \tfrac{1}{2}(M + S)$$

or

$$2A = M + S$$

Table 10.2 M signals

Microphone system	M signal
Figures-of-eight at 90°	Figure-of-eight
Hypercardioids at 90°	Cardioid
Cardioids at 90°	Poor cardioid (i.e. at 180° the response is not zero)
Cardioids at 180°	Omnidirectional

(It's normal, if slightly improper, to omit the '2' and simply write A = M + S.) With only an A signal there are equal amounts of M and S, but the mono listener won't receive the S component, so there is again something lost!

Incidentally, subtraction gives

$$B = \tfrac{1}{2}(M - S)$$

or, commonly but again improperly,

$$B = M - S$$

A postscript about terminology: here we have used A and B for left and right, and this is common practice in the professional world. However, common does not mean 'universal'. L and R for left and right can be encountered and in the non-professional field they *are* universal. To confuse matters further, in many coincident pair units X and Y are often used instead of A and B.

M/S microphones

Since A and B signals can be converted quite easily to M and S and vice versa there is obviously no reason why a coincident pair of microphones should not take the form of an M and S pair instead of being an A and B pair. Instead of two microphones angled on either side of the centre line, with an M/S pair the M microphone points forward and the S microphone (which must be a figure-of-eight) faces left and right.

There are some advantages in an M/S pair. One is that, for television use when the microphone pair is in a boom, it is helpful for the operator to have one microphone pointing at the action, as with a mono microphone in a boom. Also, the M microphone's output is automatically the mono signal for the listeners not equipped for stereo.

Usually the M microphone is a cardioid or a hypercardioid and image width can be controlled from the relative gains in the M and S channels. There have been some almost certainly exaggerated claims for M/S systems. Suggestions of better sound quality, for example, probably arise from better microphones rather than from the fact that they were in the M/S rather than the A/B mode!

Headphones and stereo

We said earlier in this chapter that a stereo effect can only occur if each of the listener's ears receive the sounds from *both* loudspeakers. From that it would appear that headphones cannot produce a stereo effect. This of course isn't true. There *is* an impression of stereo, but exactly what process is occurring isn't obvious. What can be said is that the positions of the stereo images using headphones are not in general the same as the positions perceived with loudspeakers. Much of the time this may not matter, and if the listener with headphones enjoys the experience then all is not lost. There may, however, be times when the imaging is important – in some stereo drama in radio, for example.

There is a technique which attempts to remedy the situation, what it known as *binaural stereo*. The argument here is that if a head with microphones in place of the ears were in the studio, and each microphone were connected to the corresponding earpiece of the listener's headphones then we have, in effect, moved our ears to the studio and very realistic stereo should result. It doesn't quite! What are known as *dummy head* recordings have been, and still are, made. It is possible to buy special artificial heads with cavities for microphones. An alternative, which is simpler and less likely to attract a crowd when on location, is a disc of perspex some 30 cm in diameter with small microphones mounted on the ends of a bar which passes through the centre of the disc.

Some quite impressive recordings have been made with these techniques, but unfortunately the effect for most listeners seems to be that the sounds are *behind* them. On the other hand the compatibility with loudspeaker listening is for the most part acceptable so that the occasional use of binaural stereo in broadcasting is permissible.

Transmission of stereo (radio)

Stereo transmission in the UK television system will be dealt with later after we have looked at digital processes. The stereo transmission system used in radio is basically fairly simple. First of all the A and B signals are converted into M and S. Figure 10.13 shows the essentials.

The addition is performed by adding the outputs of two amplifiers, the subtraction by reversing the phase of one signal and then adding. The M signal is transmitted normally, and this means that any mono receiver will detect it without trouble.

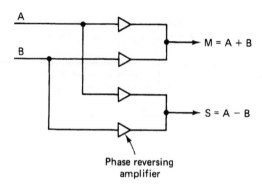

Figure 10.13 Conversion of A and B into M and S

The S signal is used to amplitude modulate a 38 kHz carrier. This results in sidebands having frequencies which are 30–15 kHz *above* 38 kHz and the same band *below* 38 kHz. That is, the S signal now consists of a range of frequencies, as shown in Figure 10.14.

The carrier frequency itself (38 kHz) is now of little immediate use. It does not convey any useful programme information and merely uses up power. It is therefore suppressed. But a stereo receiver needs to have accurate information about the phase and frequency of this carrier in order to demodulate satisfactorily. One might think that a very small amount of the 38 kHz could be transmitted, but a new difficulty arises. It is only 30 Hz away from the nearest sideband and it would be very difficult economically to design and manufacture filters that can separate 38 kHz from 37.97 and 38.03 kHz. The trick is to halve the 38 kHz, making 19 kHz, reduce this to a low level which can still be detected by the receiver, and slot this *pilot tone*, as it is called, into the spectrum. The receiver then uses the 19 kHz pilot tone to synchronize an internal 38 kHz oscillator which produces what is, in effect, the missing carrier. Notice that 19 kHz fits neatly into a 'green belt' between 15 kHz, the highest audio frequency, and 23 kHz, the lowest sideband. The 4 kHz separation is ample for the receiver to be able to filter out the suppressed carrier.

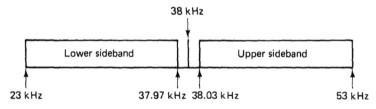

Figure 10.14 The S signal frequencies after modulation

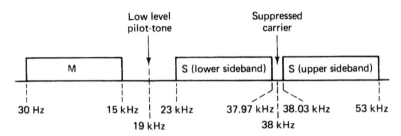

Figure 10.15 The composite audio signal

The composite S signal is then added to the M signal before being fed into the transmitter, the complete audio signal having the spectrum shown in Figure 10.15.

Facts about stereo

1. The ideal listening position is at an apex of an equilateral triangle, the loudspeakers being at the other two points. Curious imaging is apt to occur if the listener is closer than this.
2. Satisfactory listening occurs further back, provided the listener stays on the centre line.
3. The listening room should be acoustically symmetrical about an axis formed by the centre line between the loudspeakers.
4. Where appropriate the colour *red* is used to denote the A channel, *green* the B channel. (The red and green navigation lights on a ship indicate port (left) and starboard (right) respectively.)
5. What we have said in 4 above does not apply to headphones! Red is used to indicate the right earpiece.
6. *Ambisonics*, a technology designed to produce 'surround sound', has led to a particular microphone, the 'sound field microphone', being used for stereo. It contains four capsules and the processed output can be used to behave as a coincident pair whose polar diagrams and apparent mutual angle can be varied electrically (not mechanically). These and other parameters can be altered in real time and also, if a four-track recording is made, at a later time by feeding this recording back into the control unit.
7. A pair of figure-of-eight microphones is sometimes known as a 'Blumlein microphone' after Alan Blumlein who carried out much pioneer stereo work in the UK in the 1930s. He was unfortunately killed in World War II while carrying out tests on airborne radar systems – his plane crashed in the Forest of Dean in Gloucestershire.

11 Monitoring the audio signal

The dynamic range of an audio signal

First, what do we mean by *dynamic range?* Essentially it is the range in decibels from the very highest signal level (greatest loudness, perhaps) which exists *or can be permitted*, down to the lowest level which exists or can be permitted. The distinction between existing and permitting will become clear as we go on. Strictly we should define exactly how we are going to measure these extremes – are they peak or RMS values? What corrections are made? What reference levels are used? At this stage such niceties are likely to cause confusion so we will simply suppose that the same measuring instrument is used at both ends of the scale and that it indicates programme peaks.

In a studio or concert hall the background noise sets the lower end of the dynamic range. This is likely to be much higher in the concert hall than in the studio where we could reasonably suppose a sound level of around 10–20 dBA. The highest levels are likely to be found in music where a symphony orchestra, for instance, can manage momentary peaks of perhaps 120 dBA or even more. The dynamic range is therefore at least 100 dB. With other types of music, such as a rock concert, the highest levels may be greater than those of a symphony orchestra but the background levels will not generally be as low. So we can say that the dynamic range of an audio signal can easily exceed 100 dB.

Let us now look at items of equipment in the chain from studio through to transmitter, as in Figure 11.1.

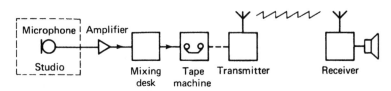

Figure 11.1 Some components in the audio chain

Microphones

The lower level is set by self-generated electrical noise and is typically around 15–20 dBA. The upper level is set by the point at which distortion occurs and this is likely to be well over 120 dBA, a range overall of at least 100 dB.

Tape machines

If these are digital we can state, without at the moment trying to explain why, that a range of 80–100 dB is feasible. Strictly we should use the term *signal-to-noise ratio*. However, this can also introduce questions of, for example, how the noise is measured and with reference to what. For clarity of understanding we'll stick to 'dynamic range', which to all intents and purposes is the same thing as far as we are concerned at the moment.

In the case of analogue – i.e. conventional – machines there is a lower limit set by tape hiss and an upper limit which is magnetic saturation of the magnetic material of the tape. The range is in the region of 50–70 dB, but depends on the width of the tracks, the tape speed and whether special noise reduction systems have been used.

The transmitter-receiver link

Again, this is very variable, being roughly 50 dB for frequency modulated radio down to about 30 dB for amplitude modulated radio (the medium and long wave bands). We could go on further, but we have said enough to show that the 100 dB or more at the studio must be reduced substantially, although with the increasing use of digital equipment in the future this reduction in the dynamic range will become less drastic than at present. How the dynamic range is reduced is another matter. One of the jobs of a sound operator sitting at a mixing desk is to control the dynamic range – that is, to bring it within acceptable limits – and in the next chapter we shall see that there are automatic devices which will perform the task very rapidly (but much less intelligently).

However, let us concentrate on the problem facing the human operator. What must be *monitored* as a first stage towards controlling the dynamic range? The answer must be, the highest levels in the programme. These are what are going to cause distortion if permissible limits are exceeded. Distortion of sound because of overloaded equipment or saturated tape is very unpleasant. Also, by definition, it is likely to be loud. If the signal is so quiet that it is getting near to the background noise levels then that is undesirable but the effect is not going to be as objectionable as overload distortion. So it is the *upper* levels of the range that need to be measured.

Zero level

Having mentioned the term 'measured' we need to establish what units of measurement we are to use. Decibels are obviously strong contenders, but what reference level should we use? The zero we met earlier when dealing with things like loudness might do, but that was based on acoustic pressures, whereas in most studio equipment we are dealing with voltages. In fact the zero that is almost universally adopted was originally based on a power of 1 milliwatt. This originated well before World War II when people regarded the power in audio circuits as being significant at all times.

1 mW is equivalent to 0 dB

Power isn't easy to measure but voltage is. Now the standard *impedance* in audio circuits is traditionally 600 ohms, because that is the characteristic impedance of an old-fashioned pair of telephone wires. (600 ohms is still important in some contexts, but much less so than formerly.) If we suppose a power of 1 mW to be dissipated in 600 ohms then because

$$W = V^2/R$$

we have, since 1 mW = 0.001 W,

$$0.001 = V^2/600$$

$$\text{or } V^2 = 0.6$$

and this gives us

$$V = 0.775\,\text{V}$$

This slightly inconvenient number then becomes the standard. It is referred to as *zero level* and is frequently written as '0 dB', provided there is no risk of confusion with the zero of the loudness scale. (0 dBu is also used, more correctly, to mean the same thing. There are many other versions with different letters appended and it can become very confusing. For simplicity we'll stick to 0 dB.)

0 dB (or 0 dBu) is also, by general agreement, taken to represent *40% of the maximum permissible signal voltage.*

We should be able to calculate how many decibels above zero level can be accepted. If 100 represents the maximum voltage and 40 represents zero level then the number of decibels difference is

$$20\log 100/40 = 20\log 2.5$$

$$= 20 \times 0.4$$

$$= 8$$

This is an important result: *zero level is 8 dB below the permissible maximum.*

We can now look at specific instruments. There are two widely-used devices which we shall deal with before mentioning other level-indicating instruments.

The VU (volume unit) meter

The VU meter is shown in Figure 11.2, and is simply a voltmeter connected across the appropriate part of the circuit. As such it does not indicate the peaks in the programme, which is really a major requirement. It does, though, have certain advantages, mainly that it is relatively cheap and also it is calibrated directly in decibels. Unfortunately the '0' mark doesn't normally mean zero

Figure 11.2 Scale of a VU meter

level. It is usually intended to indicate the maximum permissible voltage – this would correspond to 100% signal, and indeed many VU meter scales are marked in percentage as well as decibels. This would then mean that zero level corresponds to −8 on the VU scale. To confuse matters it is not unknown for different organizations to adopt different calibrations for VU meters, so all their settings need to be looked at with caution.

The PPM (peak programme meter)

This is shown in Figure 11.3.

1. The scale is white on black and there is a minimum number of markings. This helps to reduce eye strain when watching the meter for any length of time.
2. The associated circuitry causes the pointer to rise very quickly, to indicate the all-important peak voltages, and then has a slow fall-back (a few seconds). The quick rise, slow fall again makes for easier reading.

Figure 11.3 PPM

3. PPM 4 corresponds to zero level (0.775 V). This is very important.
4. There is normally 4 dB between the scale markings. (Some older PPMs had 6 dB between '1' and '2'.)
5. With 4 dB/division and PPM 4 being zero level it follows that PPM 6 corresponds to the maximum permissible voltage.
6. Although there are only a few scale markings it is possible to read to 0.5 dB, especially with steady signals.

Comparing the two types of meter it is clear that the PPM is much superior to the VU meter. It is, though, more expensive. The VU meter is, for all its limitations, reasonably satisfactory for indicating steady tones, albeit generally less accurately than the PPM. In the UK the VU meter is found principally on low-cost installations or, to take an example, on 24-track tape machines where it is adequate for setting up the machine and where it can also indicate the existence of signals going to or coming from the tracks.

It is sometimes claimed that the VU meter is a better indicator of loudness than the PPM. This is debatable. What is true is that neither device is very much good as a loudness indicator because neither makes any allowance for the ear's frequency response.

Other types of programme measuring device

Where there is little space and great accuracy is not needed various LED meters have become popular in recent years. Many of these have different coloured segments, say green for indications up to zero level or maybe +8 dB, and red for higher readings. In general the accuracy is not great – perhaps 2 dB or 3 dB per segment – but with a large number of segments better accuracy is achievable. On some LED indicators it is possible to switch from a VU characteristic to a PPM one.

A variant is to have what is sometimes called a 'bouncing ball' indication. Here the highest segment stays illuminated for a couple of seconds or so, giving a crude but quite useful indication of peaks. More expensive are *plasma* displays, in which large numbers of glowing segments are used. These can be reasonably accurate and again can be given either VU or PPM characteristics. They require a relatively large amount of electrical power.

Stereo PPMs

For monitoring stereo signals one PPM is clearly of little help. At least two, one for the A signal and one for B, are needed. Actually, no less than four are desirable because there are also the M and S signals to take into account. The M signal is the most significant as it is that which, when shown on a PPM, indicates the all-important peaks. This calls for specially designed PPMs; those most commonly used have double movements with concentric shafts to the pointers, rather like the hour and minute hands of a clock. This arrangement makes it much easier to compare the two signals than if there were a pair of side-by-side PPMs. Thus for full monitoring a pair of stereo PPMs, one for A and B and the other for M and S, are needed, although sometimes, to save space and perhaps cost, one PPM is installed and it can be switched from A/B to M/S operation. (It is quite common, even with a pair of PPMs, to have switches which change the function of each as a back-up in case of the failure of either meter.) The pointers of the meters have standard colours:

A   Red
B   Green
M   White (this is the equivalent of a mono PPM indication).
S   Yellow (presumably someone's arbitrary decision).

Interpreting stereo PPM readings

A surprising amount of useful knowledge about the stereo signal can be gained from the four pointers of a pair of stereo PPMs. Here we will merely summarize this information.

The A and B pointers

Remembering that with normal programme signals the PPM needles are constantly moving about, if the A and B pointers are weaving around the same part of the scale the probability, but not the certainty, is that the stereo images are fairly evenly balanced left and right. A prolonged period with one pointer higher than the other may mean that there is an accidental *offset* to one side.

The M and S pointers

The ratio of M and S is an indication of the *width* of the stereo image. All M means mono. All S means a totally out of phase signal. With most normal programme material the M pointer will be, on average, some 4–6 dB higher than the S pointer. Table 11.1 summarizes this.

Table 11.1 Ratio of M and S pointers

M Pointer (PPM readings)	S Pointer (PPM readings)	Likely inference
4–6	3½–4½	Normal stereo
4–6	4–6	Over-wide images. Likelihood of poor compatibility because too much S signal
4–6	2–3	Rather narrow images
4–6	1–2	Very narrow stereo
4–6	0	Mono
3–5	4–6	Large out-of-phase components
0	4–6	Totally out of phase

The reader should bear in mind that Table 11.1 is only a guide. Any of the situations, except the last, may occur in a normal stereo programme, but preferably only briefly in most cases. (Some chamber music, a string quartet for example, is often deliberately given a fairly narrow image, so the readings of M around 4–6 and S about 2–3 might not mean that something is wrong.)

12 Processing the audio signal

Equalization

Equalization (EQ) means altering the frequency response of a signal. We shall look at it as a facility used in studio operations to modify the output of microphones, tape machines and other signal sources. It is sometimes known as 'frequency correction' – but it isn't correcting any *frequencies*. 'Equalization' ought to mean making equal an imperfect frequency response and in fact it still does in some contexts, but whatever reservations one may have about the term it has come to stay in this application.

Why put 'equalization' into the flat response signal from, say, a microphone? There are many reasons, some of which we shall discuss as we go along. Just for the moment here are a few: a presenter may have a sibilant voice (the Ss are accentuated), there is annoying traffic rumble in a location recording, the ventilation system of a studio produces an undesirable whistle from one of the air outlets. All of these, and many other, undesirables in the sound signal can often (but not necessarily always) be reduced to acceptable levels by the judicious use of EQ.

The main forms of EQ which can be found on any reasonable sound desk are as follows.

Bass lift and cut

Alternative terms are 'bass boost and cut', 'LF lift and cut'. Figure 12.1 shows the effects on a flat frequency response graph of applying lift and cut at the lower end of the frequency range. Usually there are two separate controls, one for switching the 'roll-off' frequency (the frequency at which the response is 3 dB above or below normal) and the rate of the slope. This can range from zero (i.e. no effect) to a maximum which is generally about 6 dB/octave. The term 'dB/octave' refers to the rate at which the curve rises or falls when it is clear of the roll-off. (A simple capacitor–resistor circuit can be used as a bass-cut device with a slope of 6 dB/octave. The 6 dB/slope arises because the reactance of a capacitor halves as the frequency is doubled.)

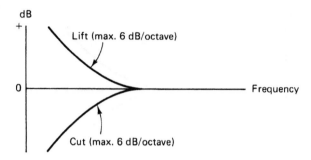

Figure 12.1 Bass lift and cut

While an operator will generally use his or her ears to decide how much EQ to use in any particular situation it is nevertheless useful to be able to carry out simple calculations. For example:

Suppose we have a recording with a very marked 50 Hz hum caused by poorly screened cables running close to the mains. We select a roll-off frequency on our equipment of 100 Hz. How effective will this application of EQ be in reducing the hum? The 6 dB/octave slope will not start at 100 Hz, but for simplicity let's suppose it does.

Then at 50 Hz the hum will be reduced by 6 dB. If the hum is severe, reducing its level by 6 dB is probably not going to be very useful. To drop the hum level by 20 dB we would need to select a crossover frequency in the region of 3–4 octaves above 50 Hz, between 400 and 800 Hz, and this will probably have very undesirable effects on the programme material.

Fortunately there are other ways of dealing with this sort of problem and we will look at them a little later.

Top lift and cut

Alternative terms are 'treble lift and cut', 'HF lift', etc. Almost everything we have said about bass lift/cut applies to top lift/cut. The simple calculation, with a few figures changed, could apply just as well.

Applications of this fairly simple type of EQ at the bass and treble ends of the spectrum are many, even if reducing mains hum is not likely to be one of them. Typical uses are:

- *Bass cut.* Reducing traffic rumble, studio ventilation, 'bassiness' in a hall or church where the low-frequency reverberation time is long.

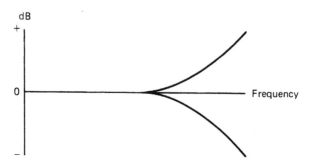

Figure 12.2 Top lift and cut

- *Bass lift.* This is generally less useful, as lifting the low frequencies introduces a risk of enhancing unwanted low-frequency sounds. It may, though, be effective in a music recording in strengthening weak bass instruments.
- *Top cut.* Reducing sibilance, high frequency whistles and possibly tape hiss.
- *Top lift.* Like bass lift this can be hazardous, but to take just one example, it may be possible to compensate to some extent for a 'dullness' caused by poor microphone positioning.

An important point about all the EQ facilities above: it can be very difficult to judge by ear what correction has been used. It can be easy to mistake bass lift for top cut, for instance, and in fact the matter can be complicated in the following way.

Suppose the operator has, for some reason, lifted the bass in an audio signal. There may now be a risk of the programme level being too high, so the overall level is taken down. The higher frequencies then actually *have* been reduced. Subjective judgements can be very misleading.

Many EQ sections of sound desks include steep bass and/or treble filters. These usually have maximum slopes of about 18 dB/octave, and a re-work of the calculation about mains hum shows that there is a chance that the hum can be markedly reduced without too much interference with the legitimate audio signal.

Presence lift and cut

This means applying a lift or cut to a band of frequencies, as represented in Figure 12.3. The term originates from an observation in the late 1950s or early 1960s that a modest lift in the frequency response around 3 kHz has the effect of making vocalists sound nearer. The reasons are obscure. The author has argued that a *cut* in the response should be called 'absence', but this hasn't caught on.

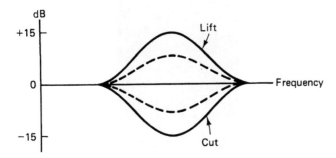

Figure 12.3 Presence lift and cut

On the more complex and expensive equipment not only the centre frequency and 'height' of the lift or cut is controllable but also the width. The latter control is often called 'Q' from its similarity to the Q of a tuned circuit.

The applications of presence controls are many. Examples from a big range include making a particular instrument more (or less) prominent and reducing a whistle in a ventilation system.

If the frequency of a presence lift/cut device is continuously variable, instead of being switched in steps, the device is called a *parametric equalizer*. An immediately obvious advantage is that particular frequencies can be accurately 'tuned-out'. One good way of doing this is to set the controls to *lift* and then slowly changing the frequency until the unwanted frequency is greatly enhanced. If the control is now changed from lift to cut it will usually be found that a satisfactory reduction in the noise is effected.

There are more of less standard symbols for EQ controls. They are shown in Figure 12.4.

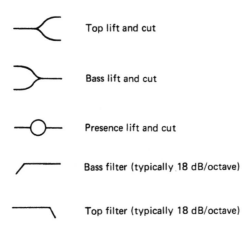

Figure 12.4 Symbols used for EQ controls

Figure 12.5 Graphic equalizer

Graphic equalizers

A *graphic equalizer* (Figure 12.5) consists of a number of narrow-band filters each of whose lift or cut is controlled by a slide potentiometer on the front panel. This means that the position of the potentiometer knobs shows approximately the frequency response graph (hence the name) which the unit is providing. There are two general types:

1. Those with 'octave filters', each control operating with centre frequencies starting with (usually) 31.5 Hz and going up in octaves (63, 125, 250, 500 Hz, etc.).
2. 'Third octave filters', in which the preferred frequencies are 25, 31.5, 40, 50, 63, 80 Hz, and so on.

The gain or loss provided by each filter is usually about ±12–14 dB.

Compressor/limiters

The distinction between compression and limiting is one which need not worry us for the moment – it is in a sense a technical rather than fundamental difference – so to begin with we shall talk about compression and add limiting later.

A compressor is an automatic gain-control device. Typical uses include reducing the gain when there are high peaks in the audio signal which might otherwise cause overloads and hence distortion, and holding the level of a particular signal at a predetermined level (which is close to the first example but not necessarily quite the same).

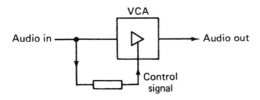

Figure 12.6 Simplified compressor

A simplified diagram to show the operation of a compressor is given in Figure 12.6. The amplifier is of a special type known as a *voltage controlled amplifier* (VCA). The important thing about it is that its gain is varied by the control voltage fed into it. Here the control signal is shown as being taken from the input, but in some types the output signal is the basis for the control. Figure 12.7 illustrates the action.

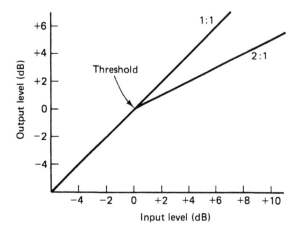

Figure 12.7 Basic action of a compressor

The vertical axis represents the *output level* and the horizontal axis the *input level*. In principle it doesn't matter much what is taken as a reference but it is usual to take standard zero level (0.775 V) as the reference. It may be helpful to remember that this is PPM 4 and that +8 is then the usual maximum normally permitted in broadcasting.

The line marked 1:1 in the diagram simply means that the equipment is not altering the ratio between input and output. This would be the case for a normal amplifier, or even a pair of wires. However, the line to pay particular attention to at the moment is the one labelled 2:1. There are two observations to be made:

1. The line diverges from the 1:1 line at a point called the *threshold*. This is adjustable and is shown here as occurring at 0 dB.
2. Above the threshold the output rises more slowly than the input. In this example, for every 2 dB increase in the input the output increases by 1 dB, hence the 2:1 label. We call this the *compression ratio*:

$$\text{Compression ratio} = \frac{\text{increase in input dB above the threshold}}{\text{corresponding increase in output dB}}$$

Figure 12.8 shows a range of compression ratios. Note that different manufacturers have different ranges of compression ratios on their products – the ones shown here are merely representative.

At this point we can introduce *limiting*. Basically this is nothing more than the limit of compression – ideally an infinite compression ratio but in practice likely to be 40:1 or more. Some compressor/limiters have separate controls for the limiter and the compressor, making it possible to have the kind of input–output

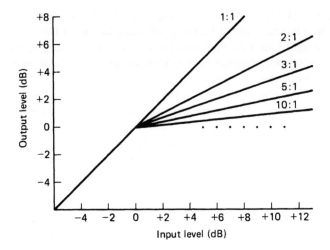

Figure 12.8 Compression ratios

characteristic shown in Figure 12.9. On others it may be found that when switching to 'limit' the threshold automatically goes to +8 dB, the theory being that this puts an immediate stop to any chance of an overload. There is quite a range of possibilities.

Besides the controls for threshold and compression ratios (or limiting) there are one or two other important parameters which should be under the control of the operator. The first of these that we will deal with is *recovery time* (also known as *release time* or *decay time*). This refers to the time that the VCA takes to return

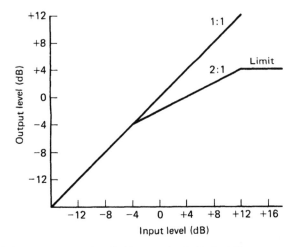

Figure 12.9 Limiting and compression; limiting at a threshold of +4 dB

to normal gain (1:1) after a sufficiently high input level has caused gain reduction to occur. In a typical unit the recovery time may be varied from perhaps 10 or 100 ms to around 3 seconds. Sometimes there is an 'AUTO' setting, which means that the recovery time depends on the duration and amplitude of the programme peak which had caused compression.

This is not the place to go into a long account of how an operator chooses recovery time settings, but we can use two examples in illustration.

1. With a short recovery time, speech (such as a commentator's voice) can 'punch' gaps into background noises so that the latter appear to be switched on and off at each pause between words. This is unnatural. A longer recovery time will probably hold the background down long enough for the effect not to occur disturbingly.
2. A long recovery time might cause speech in a news report to be held down too long after a sudden loud noise such as a gunshot. This time the gunshot would 'punch a hole' in the commentary. A short recovery time would be better.

Both of these problems can be avoided, in principle if not always in practice, by having separate limiter/compressor devices, one in the speech circuit and another in the 'effects' circuit.

A further feature of many compressor limiters is control of the *attack time*. This means the time taken by the VCA to respond to a signal level which is higher than the selected threshold. At first sight it might seem that the attack time should be extremely short so that the compression action is virtually instantaneous. In some circumstances an attack time of a millisecond or so may be desirable as it would prevent any possibility of excessive levels causing trouble. Unfortunately, though, this sudden change in the characteristics of a sound may distort the all-important starting transients and the quality of a musical instrument may thus be impaired. A long attack time – say a few tens of milliseconds – is less likely to affect the starting transients but there is a risk of peaks being distorted. The operator needs to regard attack time, threshold and compression ratio as being interdependent in their effects, and often rather delicate compromises have to be made.

Noise gates

Some compressor/limiters include a *noise gate*. The action of this is illustrated in Figure 12.10. A moment's thought will show that this is expanding the dynamic range, whereas compression and limiting reduce the dynamic range. The purpose of a noise gate is to 'push down' unwanted background noises. It may be possible, for example, to set the noise gate threshold so that all programme sound is above it. Then things like studio ventilation noise (which may, with a bit of luck, be below the threshold) will be taken down to a much lower level by the

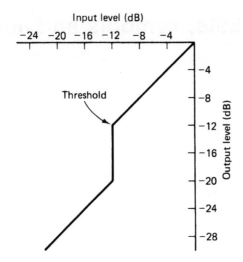

Figure 12.10 Action of a noise gate

number of decibels set by the size of the 'step'. As with all else in compressor/ limiters, noise gates have to be used with caution. Too low a threshold and the gate is ineffective; too high and the die-away of musical notes may be suddenly chopped off.

13 Sockets, symbols and amplifiers

It is appropriate here to digress slightly from the main theme of the book in order to deal with some of the symbols used in diagrams because our next topic will be sound desks, and this will make use of these symbols extensively. Secondly, a brief note about amplifiers because sound desks are full of them and here is as good a place as any to outline their functions. First, though, we'll look at a particular type of connector system.

Jacks and sockets

In the very early days of the telephone system a plug and socket arrangement was invented to allow operators to connect one subscriber to another. The design was sufficiently good for it not to have changed substantially in nearly 100 years. The plug is called a *jack* (sometimes 'Post Office jack', or 'PO jack' for short) and it is illustrated in Figure 13.1.

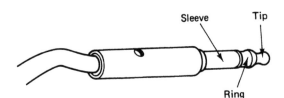

Figure 13.1 The PO jack

There are several variants: miniature ('bantam') versions are found in some equipment; there are mono and stereo versions; and it must not be forgotten that there are many connectors used in the professional world which bear no resemblance to the PO jack. But for connecting together different items of audio equipment it has few rivals and is likely to be in existence for this job for many years yet. Figure 13.2 shows the internal wiring.

There is an important difference here from usual plug and socket systems. We usually expect to find some sort of male connector at one end of a cable and a

122

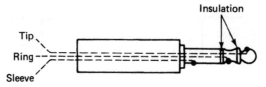

Figure 13.2 The wiring of a jack

female connector at the other end. In the case of mains connectors this is vital for safety reasons. In audio systems, though, there is normally a jack at both ends of the cable – this makes the use of such cables ('*cords*') easier. A cord with jacks at each end – the normal arrangement – is sometimes called a 'double-ender'.

The socket into which a jack is inserted is shown in Figure 13.3. Notice the *inners*, as they are called. In some circumstances these may be left unconnected.

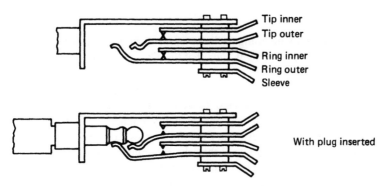

Figure 13.3 A jack socket

Alternatively they may be wired so that a programme signal passes via the socket without a jack in position, but when a jack is inserted the signal is routed through the jack. The symbol for a jack socket is ×, as in Figure 13.4.

Figure 13.4(a) implies a straightforward connection to the *outers*. In Figure 13.4(b) the line entering the × vertically (it may be from either above or below)

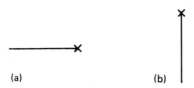

Figure 13.4 Diagrammatic representations of socket wiring

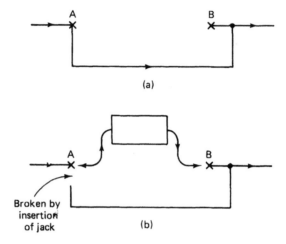

Figure 13.5 An insert point

implies that this is a wire going to the *inners*. Inserting a jack lifts the inners and in this arrangement the wiring is such that the circuit is broken, constituting what is known as a *break jack*.

To illustrate where this system, confusing to the beginner, has an application, look at Figure 13.5. The left-hand socket, A, is a break jack. The right-hand socket, B, is wired without the inners being connected. Without any jacks inserted an audio signal entering at the left emerges from the right, as in Figure 13.5(a). If a jack is plugged into B then the programme circuit is not interrupted but a pair of headphones, or other equipment, could be used to monitor the signal. The socket is then called a *listen jack*. A plug inserted into A breaks the circuit to B and the programme signal would go to whatever the plug is connected to.

An ancillary piece of equipment could be inserted here – which is why we have called it an *insert point* – as in Figure 13.5(b). There are other ways of using jacks to insert equipment and we will look at one shortly. An array of jack sockets is called a *jackfield* and one of these can be found almost anywhere in broadcasting or recording studios.

A method of connecting a piece of equipment using plugs and sockets usually requires two cords. One cord goes to the input of the equipment and one brings the output back. *Insertion jacks* manage this with only one cord. The wiring is shown in Figure 13.6. Note that a common earth wire is used and there is only one wire for each programme signal. This is what is known as *unbalanced wiring*. Care is taken with professional equipment to make sure that, to minimize the effects of induction of unwanted signals, both the programme wires are electrically equal – i.e. the wiring is balanced. The unbalanced arrangement here, though, is satisfactory provided the wiring is short and well-screened. Also, of

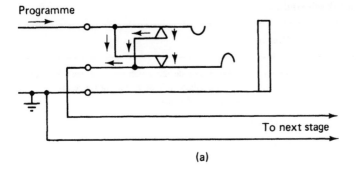

(a)

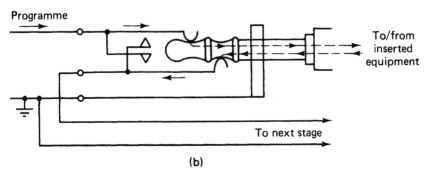

(b)

Figure 13.6 (a) Insertion jack without plug; (b) Insertion jack with plug

course, balanced equipment must be connected to a suitable transformer system to unbalance it.

Symbols

There is a full list of approved circuit symbols (British Standard 3939), but Table 13.1 shows only those that are necessary for our immediate needs. Where other pieces of equipment need to be represented we shall draw a box with an explanatory legend (or obvious abbreviation) in the box, or close to it. This is usually less confusing as it means that fewer symbols have to be memorized. In any case it's often done in the real world.

Busbar, or sometimes *bus*, means a wire used to link together many items or parts of a piece of equipment. The term will become clearer when we see examples of busbars in a sound desk. The word comes from the Latin 'omnibus', meaning 'for all'.

Table 13.1 Common circuit symbols

Symbol	Meaning
	Microphone. Based on a design which came out probably in the late 1940s. It had a spherical body and a flat gauze disk and was known as the 'apple and biscuit'.
	Loudspeaker
	Wires joining
	Switch
	Amplifier. The triangle points in the direction of the signal path. There may or there may not be a box round the triangle
dB	*Fixed attenuator (or pad).* This reduces the signal level. The number of dBs attenuation may be stated
	Resistor

Variable circuit components are shown by an arrow passing through the symbol:

Symbol	Meaning
	Variable gain amplifier. The gain may be switchable in steps of a certain number of decibels, or the control may be continuous
or (traditional)	*Fader.* The BS approved symbol shows an idealized drawing of a type of fader which went out of fashion years ago. A modern fader is essentially a variable resistor

Amplifiers

Here we are going to take what should be the material for an entire book and condense it into a very small space! To begin with this is not the place for a full account of the circuitry and electronics of amplifying devices. It must be enough to give an outline of their general types and functions.

Broadly, and to be consistent with the nature of this book, we can reduce amplifiers into two categories which we can label as *small signal* and *power* devices.

Small signal amplifiers are likely to be ones which amplify low level signals such as those from a microphone to bring them up to, typically, around zero level – to about a volt, in fact. They are frequently specified by their gain in decibels, so that it may be useful to refer, at least in diagrams, to this gain rather than specify the function as that will probably be fairly obvious from the context. Microphone amplifiers in particular will almost invariably be variable gain devices, so that they can be used with very insensitive microphones with an output in the region of −80 dB to electrostatic microphones whose output may need no more than about 50 dB amplification to bring the signal up to a useful level (which in practice may be below zero level).

Power amplifiers, on the other hand, are likely to have an input level of perhaps −10 or −20 dB and what emerges is measured not so much in dB relative to 0.775 V as watts! Obvious applications are for driving loudspeakers, which may need, typically, a minimum of about 30 W for modest monitoring loudspeakers to kilowatts (yes kilowatts!) for the speakers for a rock concert.

An important category of amplifiers of the small signal variety may not be needed to do much amplification at all, and possibly none! A good example of the zero gain type is to provide isolation between parts of a system. In Figure 13.7 the function of each amplifier is to ensure that a fault, such as a short circuit in any of the outputs, does not affect any of the other outputs. In an application such as this they are often called *distribution* amplifiers. If it seems odd to call them amplifiers it's because their circuitry is that of an amplifier but the components are chosen to make the gain either zero or possibly only a few decibels.

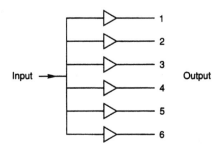

Figure 13.7 Distribution amplifiers

Two more important characteristics of amplifiers are their input and output impedances and these are chosen for the particular application. For example, if amplifiers are to be switched into a circuit it is important that their input impedances are high compared with the impedance of the circuit so that switching in or out an amplifier has a negligible effect on the voltages already in the circuit. Typically input impedances in such cases are around 10 kΩ to 20 kΩ

An example where output impedance is especially important is in loudspeaker amplifiers. Here it should normally be very low indeed, for two reasons: one, that variations with frequency in the loudspeaker's impedance will have a minimum effect, and two, there can be suitable electromagnetic damping of the coil movements.

14 Sound desks (mixing consoles)

The reason for introducing sound desks (also known as 'mixing consoles') at this stage is that we are now in a position to bring together many of the items of technology we have been looking at. The stages after a signal leaves the desk – for example, recording – can follow later.

We are going to include almost any sound-mixing equipment under this heading, from relatively simple portable mixers which can be battery-operated and are the sort of thing taken out by ENG (electronic news gathering) crews to the enormous desks used in major radio and television studios. The important point is that, with certain important exceptions, they all have the same basic structure – just as the skeletons of a horse and a mouse are basically similar each having a skull, vertebrae, and four legs with joints.

The basic functions of a sound desk

These are:

1. To amplify the weak signals from sources such as microphones, which are of the order of 1 mV (and maybe less) to bring them up to around zero level (0.775 V). At the same time the much higher outputs of tape and disk machines must also be capable of being handled.
2. To provide, where needed, means of introducing equalization, limiting and compression.
3. To allow control – adjustment of the level of each source – by means of a fader.
4. To provide access to facilities such as artificial reverberation.
5. To provide feeds of the sound signal to a studio audience and to performers, noting that these will not in general be the same as the normal output of the desk (*PA* and *foldback*).
6. To allow for the exchange of sound signals with remote studios (*clean feeds*).
7. To make it possible for different sources to be gathered into *groups* for ease of operation.
8. To allow visual and loudspeaker monitoring.

9. Provide an overall level control.
10. To allow communication with other staff and performers in the studio (*talkback*).

We shall look at each of these, in some cases combining two or more together. In doing so, though, it must be remembered that there can be exceptions to almost every statement made here. The aim is to give a not-too-complicated picture of a typical sound desk, so that if the reader were suddenly taken into a studio where a desk was being used then at least he or she would know what kind of operations were being carried out and also, later, would be able to look more closely at the labelling of the controls and find that a great deal of it was reasonably familiar. To go further than this would need another complete book.

A typical channel

By *channel* we mean here the path of an audio signal from desk input to a point where it is likely to be combined with the signals from other sources. Figure 14.1 shows the main programme path through a channel. Remember, though, that there is an enormous amount of variation in actual desks. What we are showing here, and throughout this chapter, is an idealized version which is reasonably close to most desks but shouldn't be thought of as referring to any specific one. Again, in the interests of clarity we are, for the most part, omitting amplifiers. We know that they must be present for various reasons – isolating parts of the desk from other sections, as well as to increase signal levels – but to include them in every diagram would be distracting from the main story.

There are two inputs, shown in Figure 14.1 as jack sockets, but they may be some other type of connector. The *high level* input would be suitable for the output of, say, a tape machine where the signal is likely to be around zero level. The attenuator brings this down to *microphone level*, which will be in the region of −55 to −80 dB (55–80 dB below zero level).

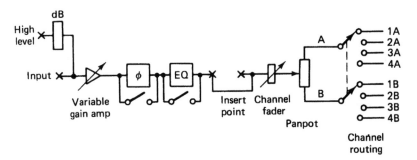

Figure 14.1 A typical channel

The variable gain amplifier allows for variations in the sensitivities of microphones or other sources to be compensated for.

The *box marked* ɸ is a *phase reversing* circuit. When it is introduced – when the by-passing switch is open – the wiring is in effect changed over so that the effects of inadvertent phase reversals in cables or equipment can be corrected.

EQ simply means that we have here a range of bass-cut/lift, top-cut/lift, presence and so on which can be switched in. (In small portable mixers this may be a very limited selection.)

The *insert point* here could, for example, allow a limiter/ compressor or maybe a graphic equalizer to be plugged in.

The *channel fader* can be used to balance the source in the channel against the sources in other channels. It can also be used to fade up or fade out a voice, say.

The *panpot* allows the source to be positioned in the stereo image. (In mono desks there will of course not be a panpot.)

From the panpot onwards there must in reality be dual wiring, double switching and double everything else, for the A and B signals. To reduce the complexity of our diagrams we are going to show just *one* route, and whether it is the A or B signal is immaterial.

Channel routing. This needs a little explanation. Remembering that a large sound desk may have 50 or more (sometimes many more!) channels it is often helpful to the operator if he or she can arrange for sources to be divided into *groups*, each of which has a fader to act as a sort of sub-master control. For example, in a musical programme there might be eight or ten microphones covering the strings, half a dozen covering the woodwind, a similar number for the brass, and so on. It would be useful if all the string channels could be sent to one group, all the woodwind channels to another and brass channels to another. Then each *group fader* could be used to balance one section of the orchestra against another with a minimum number of faders to be manipulated.

The *channel routing* unit, which is usually a set of buttons, allows each channel to be sent to any one group.

There are other parts of a channel unit – means of controlling artificial reverberation, for example. We shall deal with these later. At the moment it is the main programme path that we are concerned with.

Groups

Figure 14.2 follows on from Figure 14.1. The different wires from the channel routing buttons enter from the left and each is connected to a *group busbar*. For simplicity we have shown four groups, and indeed this might be a valid number for the smaller desks. Eight is more common on large desks.

The important parts in Figure 14.2 are obviously going to be the *group faders*. However, there may well be *group insert points*, their significance being that here

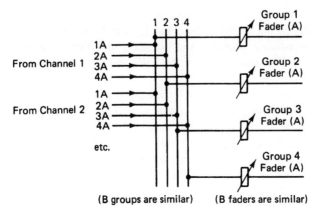

Figure 14.2 Typical groups

one item of inserted equipment could serve all the channels sent to that group. One limiter/compressor, say, could operate on all the brass instruments if necessary, whereas the alternative might mean having several limiter/compressors, one in each channel.

It is also likely that there will be provision for artificial echo control, and various other facilities in the groups, just as there is in the channels.

Output stages

Shown in Figure 14.3, the output stages are greatly simplified, like everything else we've so far dealt with in desks. But no matter – we'll put some flesh on later. First there is the busbar, which combines the outputs from each of the

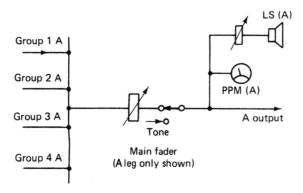

Figure 14.3 An output stage

groups. Possibly the most important item in Figure 14.3 is the *main fader*, sometimes called the *master fader*. This, it's hardly necessary to say, gives the final and over-riding control. And we have the PPM and the monitoring loudspeaker(s). The small fader in the loudspeaker circuit is simply a volume control.

There is likely to be an insert point somewhere in the output stages, to allow for an overall effect (e.g. a limiter/compressor) if needed. One feature which has sneaked in is the means of 'sending tone to line'. Built into the desk there is almost certainly going to be a very stable oscillator delivering 1 kHz (and maybe other frequencies) at an accurate zero level (0.775 V). When the tone switch is operated this *line-up tone* is (a) sent to the PPM to check that it reads '4' accurately and (b) goes on the output ('to line') so that the next stage in the system, whether a central control room, recording area or even transmitter, can check that signals are being sent and received at their correct level.

We have now seen in outline the stages that the output of, for example, a microphone pass through. The time has come to look at some of the very important peripherals.

'Echo'

Strictly we should use the phrase 'artificial reverberation', but 'echo' is shorter and easier (possibly!) to spell. We have not yet looked at the ways of generating an artificial reverberation effect, but at the moment let it suffice to say that such devices exist.

Figure 14.4 shows how a feed to the echo device may be derived. A few words of terminology first. The signal which passes straight through the desk without going to the echo device is called the *direct signal*. That which goes via the echo system is called the *indirect signal*.

There can be operational advantages in taking a proportion of the audio signal either *pre-fader* or *post-fader*. Without going into the pros and cons of why,

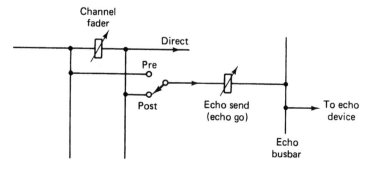

Figure 14.4 Simple echo derivation

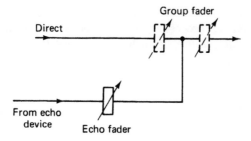

Figure 14.5 Echo return

Figure 14.4 shows how this is done. The fader marked *echo send* (or *echo go*) is likely to be a small rotary control and it allows the operator to choose the amount of the programme signal which will be reverberated. (On some desks there is a more complex arrangement called *echo mixture* which decreases the direct signal as the indirect signal is increased.) The indirect signal now goes on to a busbar where it will be joined by the echo sends from other channels.

What happens next is shown in Figure 14.5. From the echo busbar there is a connection to the echo device. There is often more than one such device and they may or may not be incorporated in the desk. The unit(s) are accessed by plugging, using jacks. Sometimes the echo units, together with other signal processing devices, are mounted in a trolley which can be placed in a convenient position by the operator.

The echo device's output goes to the *echo fader* which controls the overall indirect signal and this then joins the direct signal. The dotted lines here show that the indirect signal could join the direct either before or after the group faders. Again there are advantages and disadvantages in both. Some desks have switching which allows either.

Facts about echo

1. The echo derivation we have shown is often found in both channels and groups. In the latter case there has to be provision for ensuring that the echo return is not brought in before the same group fader – otherwise there is a risk of oscillation.
2. Large sound desks often have more than one *echo chain* so that different channels (or groups) may have different kinds of reverberation effect added.
3. There can be insert points in the echo chains to allow processing of the indirect signal, and these may be switchable to be either before or after the echo device.
4. Small PPMs for monitoring the echo go and echo return signals are often fitted.

5. The trolley we mentioned above, containing echo devices plus many other, often highly complex processing units, is generally known in the professional world as a *fairy dust trolley*. (It can be used for sprinkling magic effects on the programme signal.)

PA and foldback

These are rather similar in terms of the desk circuitry and we will consider them together.

PA stands for *public address* and in studios is really a misnomer. 'Sound reinforcement' would be more accurate. It is necessary because a studio audience will in general not hear very well what is going on. In a television sitcom, for example, if the actors' dialogue is to seem at all natural then the actors mustn't project their voices as they would in a theatre. There must then be loudspeakers in the audience area and these must be fed with *some* of the programme sound. It would be a mistake to feed them the straight output of the desk because some sources will not need reinforcing. Think of a singer with band. The audience will probably hear plenty of the louder instruments directly but the singer's voice will almost certainly need reinforcing. We shall look at the problems associated with PA in Chapter 20.

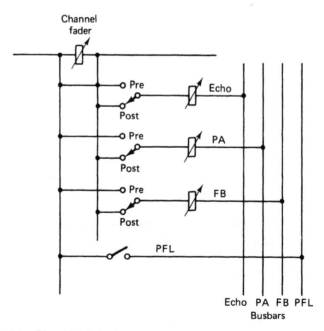

Figure 14.6 Echo, PA and FB derivation

Foldback, FB for short, is for the benefit not of the audience but of the performers. A vocalist may need to hear a reinforced sound from part of the band; a prerecorded 'backing track' also needs to be made audible for a singer; sound effects in a play might have to be heard by the actors, and so on. The foldback can sometimes be played over loudspeakers (discreet and out-of-vision ones in television and sometimes so in radio) or possibly by headphones – not usually satisfactory when in vision. Figure 14.6 is a repeat of Figure 14.4 but with the addition of the PA and FB derivations and also a thing marked PFL, which we shall deal with shortly.

A brief study of the diagram shows that the way the PA and FB signals are derived is essentially the same as for echo. The significant differences come in what happens to these signals afterwards. Instead of going to a special processing unit as the echo signal does there are master controls and then the PA and FB signals go to the loudspeakers or headphones in the studio, as appropriate. So PA and FB are simpler, in terms of the circuitry, than echo.

Facts about PA and foldback

1. The important distinction to remember is that PA is for the audience, FB is for the performers.
2. Usually PA and FB can be derived from both channels and groups, at least on large desks. Small portable mixers will generally not provide these signals – nor is there likely to be any need for them in many of the circumstances in which such mixers are used.
3. There are generally insert points in both PA and FB feeds so that processing of the signals may be carried out when necessary.
4. Both can usually be monitored. This may involve switching a PPM and a loudspeaker to whichever needs to be checked.

Pre-fade listen (PFL) and after-fade listen (AFL)

It is often vitally important for an operator to be able to monitor a signal before it is faded-up. An obvious example is in a news programme when a contribution is going to come from a remote studio, live. The far studio will use its 'send tone' facility and the desk operator will need to check the level of the tone (and maybe listen to it to make sure that it isn't mains hum!) without fading it up so that it goes out to the transmitters.

PFL is usually obtainable in two ways, first by operating a key or button which connects the busbar marked PFL in Figure 14.6 to the monitoring system, and secondly by means of special contacts in the faders which do the same job when the fader knob is pressed against its faded-out position. This is known as *overpress* and is represented diagrammatically by the symbol in Figure 14.7.

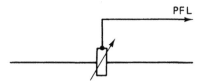

Figure 14.7 The symbol for overpress

AFL allows the signal to be monitored after the fader, and is usually operated by a separate switch or button.

Facts about PFL and AFL

1. The term *prehear* is also used to mean PFL.
2. Often a small light comes on near the PPM(s) when AFL is in use to warn the operator that it is AFL and not programme sound that is being monitored.
3. PFL and AFL are usually a facility on groups as well as channels.

Clean feed

There are many occasions when, in addition to the main output of a desk, which may be going to a transmitter or a sound or video recorder, there needs to be a second output which is an incomplete version of the main output. This second output consists of the main output *less* one or more of the sources which are going into the desk. This second output is called in the UK a *clean feed*, although the US term *mix minus* is perhaps more accurate. The technology of producing a clean feed is usually very simple – the reasons for its existence are less obvious. Let us take a few examples:

1. A musical programme originating in the UK is also being sent to another country, say Germany, where the announcements will be given in German. The desk output to the UK transmitters will consist of the music, plus of course, the English announcements. A desk output of the music only, without the English announcements, goes to Germany. This will be a clean feed, since it lacks the UK announcer's microphone input. A similar situation exists in international sporting events where the feed to the other countries will consist only of things like crowd noises.
2. Imagine a studio which has to provide an insert to a news programme originating in another studio. Its output will go straight to the main studio's desk but it is of course necessary for the contributor to hear the main studio's news reader. It will normally be undesirable if the complete main desk output returns to the remote studio, as the desk there will have the contributor's voice

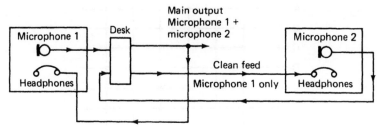

Figure 14.8 A use of clean feed

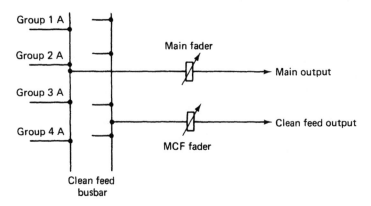

Figure 14.9 Desk output with MCF facilities

coming in along the line as well as from his microphone. The main desk will then send a clean feed which will be whatever is going into the main desk *except* the remote studio's contribution. Figure 14.8 illustrates this.

The output stages of a desk often include a separate fader for controlling the level of the clean feed output. This is sometimes labelled the *main clean feed* (MCF) fader. Figure 14.9 shows a modification of Figure 14.3 which includes it. In general all inputs to the desk will go to the main output. Only those which are to constitute the clean feed will go to the MCF busbar.

Multiway working

A news or current affairs programme of only moderate complexity is quite likely to need to link together several studios in different parts of the country, or even the world. This means that there may well be a need for multiple clean feeds so that several contributors can join in a discussion. This involves the use of a

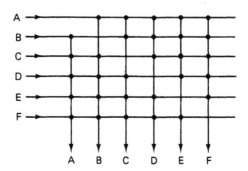

Figure 14.10 Multiway working matrix

multiway working matrix (MMW). This is easier than it sounds. Figure 14.10 should help.

All the sources, A to F, are fed into the matrix on the left. The corresponding outputs back to each source appear at the bottom. Notice that the wiring is arranged so that source A does not appear in output A, and so on. In other words each source receives all outputs except its own. (The existence of a blob implies a connection between the crossing wires.)

Deriving mono from stereo

We put this topic here because we are referring to desk outputs, where a mono output is perhaps almost as important as the stereo one. A clean feed to a remote studio will almost certainly be mono, the mono signal needs, as we have seen, to be checked for compatibility, and there may be other reasons.

Because $M = A + B$ it might seem as if all that has to be done is to combine the A and B signals. Not quite! Suppose we have both A and B signals peaking 6 on the PPM. What is the M signal going to peak? It will depend on the *coherence* of the A and B signals – in other words, are A and B equal in every respect (as in mono), in which case they are described as being *coherent*, or are they totally un-related, when they are said to be *non-coherent*? Suppose that A and B are coherent (Figure 14.11). The voltages are at all times the same, so that their addition will give an output 6 dB higher. If A and B both read PPM 6 then the M PPM will indicate 7½, 6 dB over the top!

If A and B are non-coherent but reading PPM 6 then what the M PPM will show will depend on just how non-coherent A and B are. (If they are completely out of phase their addition will be zero.) There is thus a dilemma.

The general solution has been to put an attenuator (or *pad*) in the M signal, as in Figure 14.12. The next question is what attenuation should be used? Here,

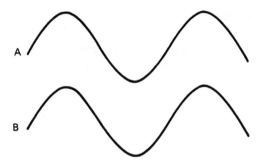

Figure 14.11 Coherent signals

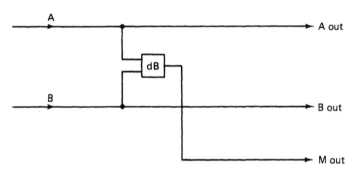

Figure 14.12 Deriving M from A and B

different organizations adopt different values, for example 3 dB, 4.5 dB or 6 dB.

While the pad gets us out of trouble in the main problem, it can introduce other nuisances. The principal one is in the matter of zero level line-up tone, which we mentioned earlier in this chapter. As an example, suppose the pad has an attenuation of 3 dB. Should this indicate 4 on the M PPM, or the A and B PPMs, or all three? If the latter, how can it do so with the pad in place? The answer has to be that it must read 4 correctly on the M PPM, so the A and B PPMs will read 3 dB lower: '3¼'. This means, as we go backwards down the chain, that *stereo line-up tone* should be, in this case, 3 dB lower than zero level, i.e. at −3 dB. And if the pad is 4.5 dB, 6 dB or any other value, there have to be corresponding corrections.

This may seem rather confusing. If it's any consolation, it has caused confusion to countless thousands of professionals in the broadcasting world in the early stages of their careers − and sometimes in the later stages!

Communications

One of the least glamorous but at the same time most important part of any studio's technology is the provision of internal communications. This is important enough in a radio or recording studio but is even more so in television. It is perhaps history rather than logic which usually puts studio communications into the province of the sound department. We can outline briefly the nature of these vital links. The most important facility is *talkback* – a means of speech communication between control room and studio plus, often, other areas. The nature of the talkback system varies significantly between radio and television, so we will deal with these separately.

Radio and recording

The producer and the sound operator have microphones which may be fed into the studio, to a loudspeaker and/or headphones when a key or button is pressed. The main purpose is to allow directions to be given to the performers. In *rehearsal conditions* it will normally be the loudspeaker in the studio which is used, but when the studio is either on the air or a recording is being made (*transmission conditions*) headphones are obviously the only safe means of communication. A *rehearsal/transmission switch* carries out the appropriate changeover automatically at the same time as controlling red 'On Air' lights. Other areas may also be linked with the talkback system – for example, recording areas and other studios.

Television studios

The talkbacks (note the plural) are much more complicated. To begin with, the director/producer's talkback instructions are, for the most part, to the technical staff – camera crew, lighting and sound staff. The *production talkback* microphone is normally live all the time as the instructions tend to be continuous. Also the recipients are wearing headphones. (*Loudspeaker talkback* to the entire personnel of the studio exists but is much less used – for obvious reasons.) Instructions to performers are generally conveyed by a floor manager who carries a small radio receiver which picks up the production talkback.

The sound operator (generally called the *sound supervisor* in television) will, like the lighting director and others, also have access to the production talkback but only when a key or button is operated. The sound supervisor will, however, have his or her own talkback to certain of the sound crew in the studio.

Finally, in this very incomplete account, we should mention *reverse talkback*, applicable to both radio and television. It is a means of allowing people in the studio to talk to the production staff – a sound boom operator may wish to consult his supervisor about the exact positioning of the boom microphone, for instance. Such conversations are likely to be frowned on when recording is in progress!

Computer assisted mixing (CAM)

This is a vastly complicated subject and can be given no more than an outline here. Briefly, there are two main uses for a computer when coupled to a sound desk:

1. To store in its memory information about settings of the desk controls – particularly the faders – and recall this information when required.
2. To control one or more tape machines – one of these being generally a multi-track machine.

The use of CAM in live broadcasting is very limited indeed. Its main use is with popular music, television post-dubbing (laying the sound, including effects, after the pictures have been shot and edited) and increasingly with radio drama, all of these being operations where the laying of many signals on a 24-track tape machine can be helpful. It is mainly in the mixing stage (*mix-down*) where the various tracks are combined together that the computer is useful. We must emphasize that the computer does no more than assist. It cannot make any decisions about the timing or the balance of the sounds which have been recorded – the day when a computer can do that is a very long way off, much to the relief of sound operators throughout the world.

Taking the first use – storage of desk control settings – this allows, for example, a complex build-up of the tracks to be done in stages. In real-time working all of the faders have to be manipulated together at all times. Here, the computer can store the fader movements, if necessary a few at a time. Or a complicated sequence can be worked on and stored. In either of these cases the operator can command the computer to join together two separate sequences. Alternatively the stored settings may be 'updated' by adjusting the faders. In some systems the faders are driven by small servo-motors under the control of the computer, the operator automatically being given control the instant the fader knobs are touched. In other systems fader movements are added by the computer to the stored settings. Also it may be possible to select the best of a number of trial mixes and automatically join this on to other mixes. The list of options is almost endless.

The other main use is for the computer to control the multi-track and other tape machines. These need to have one track carrying timing information ('time code'), a topic we will deal with later. The computer can locate quickly and accurately specified points on a tape, start or stop at other specified points, run two or more machines in synchronism and put in 'offsets' where needed so that one machine can run deliberately out-of-step with, but at the same speed as, another machine. These facilities are particularly useful in 'post-dubbing' operations in television.

Assignable facilities

Again, an advanced topic for which there can be only a mention here. A large modern sound desk may have several thousand controls and very many of these are replicated. There may, for example, be 50 or more sets of EQ controls. The basic idea of assignability is that there could be only one or two sets of complete controls but the operator can *assign* these to any channel or group at the press of the appropriate button. A computer stores the settings, which means that the same controls can then be assigned to another channel. Channels which need to have, say, the same EQ settings for stereo can have one lot of settings 'copied' to the other channel(s), thus saving the need to adjust accurately all the controls twice.

15 Digital audio

So far we have been dealing with audio signals in which the electrical voltage is as far as possible a replica of the original sound waves – the voltage is an *analogue* of the sound waves. Analogue signals are prone to errors. In tape recording, for example, it is difficult to ensure that the magnetization of the tape is an exact analogue of the sound signal. Also the background noise caused by the magnetic particles on the tape is an undesirable addition, albeit quite often a minor one, and multiple copying of a tape causes rapid degradation. Any form of radio transmission introduces further impairments. All of these additional effects, whether they be noise or just a distortion of the original, cannot be separated out from the wanted analogue signal. In *digital audio* the analogue signal is converted into pulses of voltage, which *can* be distorted and generally interfered with but, as long as they can be identified as some sort of a pulse, can be regenerated and consequently converted back into a good analogue signal.

Sampling

The first step in obtaining a digital signal is to *sample* the analogue signal. This means measuring its amplitude at frequent intervals. The useful audio frequency range used in broadcasting, it will be remembered, is 30 Hz to 15 kHz. It should be clear that the sampling process must occur at least 15 000 times a second. That actually is not enough – the sampling frequency must be at least *twice* the highest audio frequency. To understand why, look at Figure 15.1.

On the left a 15 kHz signal is sampled at 15 kHz. There is one sample per cycle and the height of each sample is the same. The sample height (amplitude) gives no information to suggest that there is even an audio signal there. In the right-hand diagram, sampling of the same signal is taking place at twice the 15–30 kHz. There is now a distinct difference between samples. A generally accepted rule for the sampling frequency f_s is

$$f_s = 2.2 \times f_{max}$$

where f_{max} is the highest audio frequency to be sampled. It may be surprising that only two samples for each audio cycle, as in Figure 15.1, can be acceptable –

Figure 15.1 Sampling at the highest audio frequency

they don't appear to give any information about the shape of the audio signal. Remember first that we are at the moment looking at 15 kHz. Now the difference between a sine and a square wave is simply a matter of harmonics. The square wave at 15 kHz consists of sine waves of 15, 45, 75 kHz, etc. (see Chapter 4). But the human ear can't detect anything above, at best, 20 kHz, so it certainly cannot be aware of 45 kHz and higher. In other words the ear cannot tell the difference between sine waves and square waves at 15 kHz. In fact, simple tests show that listeners cannot normally tell the difference between sine waves and square waves above about 7 or 8 kHz. Figure 15.2 represents the sampling process at a much lower frequency than in Figure 15.1, 1 kHz, say.

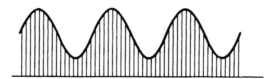

Figure 15.2 Sampling

If the samples are close enough together – or frequent enough – it should then be possible to have sufficiently accurate information for the original analogue signal to be reproduced very faithfully. If we assume the highest audio frequency we deal with is 15 kHz then the sampling frequency should be at least 2.2 × 15 kHz = 33 kHz. This sampling frequency is used, as we shall later see, but is no longer one of the universal standards. For reasons too complicated to set out here, the universal standards are now 44.1 kHz and 48 kHz; 44.1 kHz is sometimes regarded as a 'domestic' standard and 48 kHz the professional standard, but much professional equipment operates at 44.1 kHz so the distinction is not very valid.

Quantizing

It is all very well saying that we must measure the audio signal very frequently; what we have yet to specify is the degree of accuracy with which the

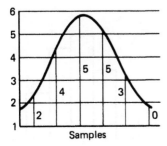
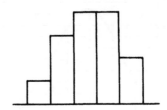

Figure 15.3 Digitizing with poor accuracy

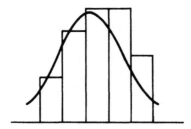

Figure 15.4 The origin of quantizing noise

measurements are to be made. Figure 15.3 shows this measurement with poor accuracy.

In the diagram there are only six measurement levels, which we shall call *quantizing levels*. The decoded signal will appear as on the right, consisting of a set of steps of varying height, and in Figure 15.4 we see this stepped signal superimposed on the original.

The stepped waveform in Figure 15.4 is really the original with the addition of 'blips' above and below it. These blips are obviously a form of noise. This is called, not surprisingly, *quantizing noise*. It has a peculiar quality when listened to, the best description being 'granular'.

At this point you are entitled to wonder what is going on! We are trying to find a way of avoiding distortion and noise and immediately invent a system which introduces a new and disagreeable noise. The fact is that background noise in an audio (or, for that matter, video) chain is always going to be present. What is important is that the noise level is low enough not to matter – or the *signal-to-noise ratio* is good enough. In this case what we have to do is to make the steps in the reproduced waveform so small that the quantizing noise is inaudible. This could be done in two ways: increase the sampling frequency, which is possible but is impracticable for reasons which we will see later, or increase the number of quantizing levels. It is the latter which is the more satisfactory answer.

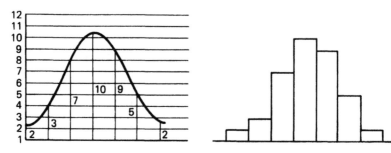

Figure 15.5 Doubling the number of quantizing levels

Imagine we double the number of quantizing levels, as in Figure 15.5. If the number of levels is doubled the step size is halved and consequently the noise blips are also halved in amplitude. Thus the noise will then be reduced by 6 dB. A further doubling of the number of levels gives a further 6 dB improvement and so on. Table 15.1 shows the basic relationship between the number of levels and the resulting signal-to-noise ratio. (The latter figure is capable of being expressed in a number of ways and the figures given here may differ slightly from others that you may see quoted. It depends on what method of measurement is used. This doesn't matter as far as a basic understanding is concerned.)

The next question is, what signal-to-noise ratio is acceptable? It depends on circumstances. Obviously the higher the better, but there can be penalties in cost and complexity. Let us simply state at the moment that for the distribution of high quality radio signals to transmitters around 65–70 dB is reasonable – about 8000 levels; for good quality recordings, as with compact discs, 65 000 levels are needed.

To summarize, the audio signal is going to be sampled some 30 000 to 50 000 times a second, and each sample is going to be measured with a scale having at least 8000 graduations on it, preferably about 65 000. It is clearly not very practicable to try to handle, say, 44 000 measurements a second, each being a number between 0 and 65 000! The arithmetic needs simplifying.

Table 15.1

Number of quantizing levels	Signal-to-noise ratio (dB)
64	25
128	31
256	37
1 024	49
4 096	61
8 192	67
32 768	79
65 536	85

Bits (binary digits)

Binary arithmetic is an arithmetic based on 2, unlike our normal arithmetic which is based on 10. Without going into a complete explanation we can simply show, in Table 15.2, the relation between binary and decimal numbers.

Table 15.2

Decimal number	Binary number
0	0
1	1
2	10
3	11
4	100
5	101
6	110
7	111
8	1000
9	1001
10	1010

A binary number such as 110010 is analysed as follows:

$$
\begin{array}{cccccc}
1 & 1 & 0 & 0 & 1 & 1 \\
2^5 + & 2^4 + & 0 + & 0 + & 2^1 + & 0 \\
= 32 + & 16 + & 0 + & 0 + & 2 + & 0 \\
= 50
\end{array}
$$

The whole point about binary numbers in this context is that we can think of a number such as the one above, consisting of 1s and 0s, as representing a voltage 'on' or 'off'. In fact it is a sequence of pulses, as in Figure 15.6.

Perhaps the reader can now see where this is leading to. Pulses can be distorted very severely but they can still be identified as pulses. In fact, providing they are not too far gone they can be used to trigger a pulse generator which will produce brand-new pulses. Figure 15.7 compares analogue and digital signals in this respect.

1 0 1 1 0 1 0 0 0 1 0 1 0 1 1 0 1 0

Figure 15.6 A binary number represented by pulses

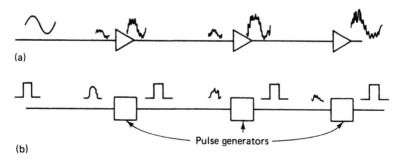

Figure 15.7 Effects of degradation of (a) analogue and (b) digital signals

Any attempt at restoration of an analogue signal is more or less bound to preserve any noise and distortions which may have crept in, whether caused by a recording/reproduction process or by impairments introduced over a long signal path – transmission and reception perhaps. Digital signals can be regenerated, however, not quite indefinitely but almost.

Let us return now to the use of binary arithmetic as a code for the very large numbers needed to represent sample amplitudes. We speak of, say, a '10-bit system' meaning that ten binary digits are needed to represent the sample amplitude. We can add another column to our first table (see Table 15.3).

The number of quantizing levels is given by 2^n where n is the number of bits and the approximate signal-to-noise ratio is $(6n-11)$ dB. While 16 bits is sufficient for broadcasting and the table could stop there, improvements in technology are making it possible for more than 16 bits to be usable in other areas.

Table 15.3

Number of quantizing levels	Number of bits	Signal-to-noise ratio (dB)
64	6	25
128	7	31
256	8	37
1 024	10	49
4 096	12	61
8 192	13	67
32 768	15	79
65 536	16	85
262 144	18	97
1 048 576	20	109

Bit-rate (bits per second)

This is of great importance in deciding the parameters of a digital system. It is calculated from

Sampling frequency × number of bits/sample

Thus a 10 bit system using 32 kHz sampling will have a bit-rate of 10 × 32 000 = 320 kb/second. This might appear to be the *bandwidth* required but in fact this is not quite so. To begin with, the highest frequency present in a digital signal occurs when 1s and 0s alternate; 101010101 has a higher frequency component than 1100110011 (Figure 15.8).

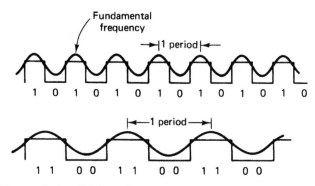

Figure 15.8 Frequencies in a digital sample

In Figure 15.8 the sine wave which is the fundamental of the 10101010 sample takes up the time for *two* digits, so the fundamental frequency is *half* the bit-rate. To complicate matters the square waves of the digital sample consist of not just the fundamental but harmonics of that frequency: 3 times, 5 times and so on.

All this means that the *bandwidth* needed for a digital system is not easy to calculate, but the bit-rate can be taken as an indication of the sort of bandwidth which will be needed.

Notice that with digital audio we are having to deal with far higher frequencies than in analogue systems. The maximum we need to worry about in analogue is 15 kHz; in the region of 320 kHz is needed for a fairly modest digital system. And to be more ambitious, a 16-bit system with 44.1 kHz sampling needs rather more than 700 kHz! (And that's for mono. Stereo needs over 1400 kHz.)

We can return for a moment to an observation we made earlier in this chapter when we said that the step size in the reproduced signal could be reduced by either increasing the sampling frequency or increasing the number of quantizing levels, but the former was not very practical. To improve the signal-to-noise ratio by 6 dB we have to halve the step size. If we double the number of quantizing levels we increase the number of bits by only 1, so the bit-rate goes up by a relatively small amount. To double the sampling frequency from, say, 44 kHz to 88 kHz would *double* the bit-rate. This is why we said earlier that increasing the sampling frequency was not a practical way of significantly improving the signal-to-noise ratio.

Error detection

One advantage of digital systems is that it is possible to detect and even correct errors which creep into the bit-stream. This is virtually impossible with any analogue system.

The subject of error detection and correction is a very complex one if gone into in depth. Here we shall do no more than give an outline of the principles. The simplest system uses what is known as *parity*.

Parity

We shall refer to the analogue-into-digital part of a system as the 'encoding' end of the chain and the reverse process as the 'decoding' end. At the encoding stage the number of 1s in the sample is counted and, if necessary, made up to an even number by adding a *parity bit*. Table 15.4 illustrates this, using a 10-bit system for simplicity.

At the decoding end the number of 1s is again counted – it should be an even number. An odd number of 1s means that either a 1 has been lost or a 0 has been created spuriously. One possible course of action used in many systems is to repeat the previous sample, which has been stored in case of this contingency. The likelihood of the repetition of samples only 1/30 000 or less of a second apart being detectable to the ear is very small.

The fallacy in using simple parity is that *two* errors, or any even number of errors, will not be detected. In practice, though, with any well-designed system

Table 15.4 Parities

Sample	Number of 1s	Parity bit needed?	Sample with parity bit
1101001101	6	No	11010011010
1011001111	7	Yes	10110011111
0001010001	3	Yes	00010100011
1110111011	8	No	11101110110

b_1	b_2	b_3	b_4	p_1
b_5	b_6	b_7	b_8	p_2
b_9	b_{10}	b_{11}	b_{12}	p_3
p_4	p_5	p_6	p_7	

Figure 15.9 Multiple parity

the chances of double errors occurring frequently are very small indeed. For broadcasting purposes a double error every quarter of an hour, say, is not likely to be very objectionable when many domestic receivers produce a click when refrigerator doors are opened or the central heating switches on.

We have described *even parity*, where the number of 1s in each sample is made up to an even number. Some digital equipment uses *odd parity*, making the number of 1s up to an odd number.

A further, much more complex, parity system can not only detect errors but even correct them. Suppose, for ease of explanation, we have a 12-bit digital system. In Figure 15.9 the 12 bits are set out in a 4 by 3 matrix: b_1, b_2, b_3, etc. are the bits in the sample; p_1 is a parity check on row 1, p_2 on row 2, p_3 on row 3, while p_4 checks on *column* 1, and so on. Supposing bit 6 should be a 1 and is corrupted to become a 0. This will be shown by the parity checks on row 2 and column 2, thus identifying the exact error. If a 0 has been received then this is wrong and a 1 can be created and inserted. These extra parity bits do, of course,

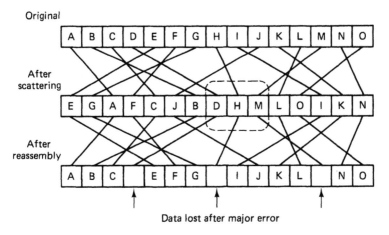

Figure 15.10 A scatter code (the dashed rectangle represents a major error)

take up space – increasing the number of bits per second, for instance. They may literally take up space: some 30% of the working area of a compact disc is taken up with error correction!

Scatter codes

A further error detection system can be mentioned briefly. The samples in an encoded signal are distributed over a relatively wide range (of time, on tape or on the disk, for example) using a special code. In the event of a major error – a lack of oxide on the tape perhaps – then, when the samples are reassembled correctly, the error is made much less serious and there is a likelihood that parity checks will restore the lost information.

A scatter code is shown in Figure 15.10.

16 Further digits

One of the most useful things about digits, apart from the better audio signal quality which can result, is that pulses can be manipulated, moved around, compressed in time, reversed, and so on. In this chapter we shall look at some of the ways in which these processes are used.

Time division multiplex (TDM)

Probably the best way of explaining this is to give an example. In the UK the BBC has the problem of distributing several radio networks to a large number of transmitters. One possibility (a costly one) would be to have separate 'circuits' (cables or radio links) for each network, not forgetting that each will need to carry dual signals for stereo. The principle of the system that is used is shown, very much simplified, in Figure 16.1.

Figure 16.1 A TDM system

Radio 1 is indicated by R1, Radio 2 by R2 and so on. Stereo left and right signals are represented by (A) and (B). Each block in the diagram represents *one sample*. To allow the system to work in real time or as close to it as possible, each one of the original samples has to be compressed so that the entire set of compressed samples – we will use the word *frame* – only occupies the time for one original sample (in this case 1/33 000 second, 33 kHz being the sampling rate used). The 'squeezing' of the original samples can be thought of as a process of putting each bit into a store and then 'reading' the contents of the store very rapidly. At the decoding end accurate timing, aided by special 'marker' pulses, allows each network's samples to be separated out from the complete frame. If each compressed sample is stored, briefly, and then read out more slowly the samples are expanded to their original durations. We must add that Figure 16.1 shows only a part of the real frame. Up to about 18 separate sets of signals can be handled – eight for the main networks and up to ten additional ones for special purposes such as internal data links. Thus time division multiplex means a period of *time* is *divided* in order to *multiplex* several signals – that is, to combine the different signals in such a way that they all occupy only one signal path.

Bit-rate reduction

We have already seen that the bandwidths needed for digital signals are far greater than for their analogue equivalents. We shall continue to use the bit-rate (bits or kilobits per second) as a rough indication of the bandwidth involved. Thus, any way of reducing the bit-rate is bound to be advantageous. A system used in the UK is known as NICAM, which stands for Near Instantaneous Companding Audio Multiplex. It was devised to reduce the number of bits in the radio distribution network outlined above (see Time division multiplex). This is an outline of how it works. (There are two versions of NICAM. We shall look at the second one later.)

The object is to reduce, say, 14 bits to 10, without any detectable impairment in the quality of the audio signal. The stages in the operations are:

1. The analogue audio signal is sampled and digitized into 14 bits.
2. Blocks of 32 samples are examined to find the largest sample present in the 32. NICAM is described as *near-instantaneous* because there is naturally a small delay in finding the largest of 32 samples. Even so, this is small because the sampling frequency used is 32 kHz, so the delay is only about 1 millisecond. (Other system delays bring the total up to several milliseconds.)
3. The amplitude of the largest sample is used to decide which of five *ranges* will be used. Figure 16.2 helps to show what that means.

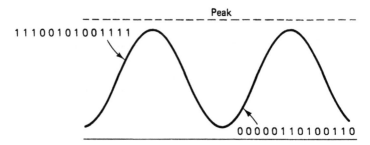

Figure 16.2 NICAM ranges

The sample near the top of the waveform might be something like

1 1 1 0 0 1 0 1 0 0 1 1 1 1

The *range* in this case will involve using only the first ten bits and neglecting the last four bits:

| 1 1 1 0 0 1 0 1 0 0 | 1 1 1 1 |
drop

This might seem rather drastic, but with ten bits the signal-to-noise ratio is still around 49 dB (see Chapter 14), and if the signal amplitude is large it can be assumed that any noise will be masked.

Now let us look at a sample near the bottom end of the waveform, which is of course, 'quiet'. The sample now might look like:

0 0 0 0 0 1 1 0 1 0 0 1 1 0

The range now will mean taking the *last* ten bits, and dropping the first four, which, because the amplitude is small, will be 0s anyway.

0 0 0 0 | 0 1 1 0 1 0 0 1 1 0 |
drop

The five ranges, then, can be represented by the following, the boxed digits being the ones that are actually used.

| 1 1 0 1 1 0 1 0 0 1 | 0 1 1 0

0 | 1 0 0 1 1 1 0 1 0 1 | 1 0 1

0 0 | 1 1 0 1 1 0 0 0 1 0 | 1 0

0 0 0 | 1 1 1 1 0 1 1 0 1 0 | 1

0 0 0 0 | 1 0 0 1 1 0 0 1 1 1 |

Extra digits (the *range code*) have to be sent, naturally, to tell the decoding end which range is being used so that 0s can be inserted at the correct places to make up the fourteen bits. However, very few digits are needed for this as the maximum number is only five and they need to be sent only once with every 32 samples. Overall the bit-rate of the original signal is markedly reduced and there are no audible ill-effects.

Data compression

This is a continuation of the bit-rate reduction process but some methods work in such fundamentally different ways from the process we have just described that it is convenient to have a new title. Essentially the idea is to mimic as closely as possible the human hearing characteristics. To begin with there is a large range of sound wave levels and frequencies which are inaudible. (This is sidestepping the point that if waves are inaudible we shouldn't call them *sound* waves!) A quick glance at Figure 3.3 on page 17 shows that for example frequencies below 50 to 100 Hz need to be at quite a high sound pressure to be audible. Yet such waves are going to be present in very many recording situations. If the system can be made to ignore them then immediately there will be a saving in the information that has to be handled.

A further saving results from a curious property of the hearing system known as *noise masking*. This is a rather complicated thing to explain but briefly it means that a tone of particular level can render the ear totally insensitive to other tones of lower level and adjacent (mostly higher) frequency. We should emphasize that this is not the same thing as a loud noise simply swamping all other noises. It's much more subtle.

To summarize, this kind of data compression, often called PASC (Precision Adaptive Subband Coding) and also referred to sometimes as *perceptual coding*, can result in dramatic reductions in the number of bits to be transmitted or recorded. It is possible to throw away up to 80% of the original digital data and the ear can still find the results acceptable. This technique makes possible such things as MiniDisc, where magnetic discs similar to those used for computer data storage can compete with CDs in recording duration if not perhaps in quality, although the degradation may be difficult to detect.

Basic sound-in-syncs (SiS)

This was developed by the BBC about 1970 and has since come into use with several other UK networks. The object is to have one carrier system for both vision and sound signals for distribution to transmitters. It is in effect a time division multiplex arrangement, but it is unusual in that it multiplexes analogue (the vision) and digital (the audio) signals. Basically the digitized audio signal is carried in the part of the video waveform which is normally reserved for line synchronization. Figure 16.3 shows this.

The 'line sync pulse' is the information which tells all receivers, monitors and cameras to start scanning a new line. In the UK television system there are 625 lines for each complete picture and 25 complete pictures per second, resulting in 15 625 lines per second and hence this number of sync pulses each second. The basic processes involved are:

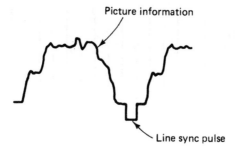

Figure 16.3 A typical television line

1. The television sound signal is sampled at a rate of 31 250 kHz. This peculiar number is actually twice line frequency, 15 625 kHz. This means that there are exactly two samples per line. Quantizing is carried out to a 10-bit standard. This may not seem very good, but in fact a companding process is carried out. The audio signal is compressed before sampling and expanded after conversion back to analogue and this makes the signal-to-noise ratio equivalent to slightly better than a 12-bit system.
2. The 'mid-line' digital sample is stored for a half line duration so that it can be fitted into the sync pulse period, as in Figure 16.4.
3. The two samples are interleaved and this operation is illustrated in Figure 16.5. The reason for interleaving is given in the next paragraph.
4. One of these two samples is inverted – 1s become 0s and vice versa. There is, not surprisingly, a good reason for this. The sync pulse area is a slightly sensitive one in that fluctuations in the mean voltage there could cause

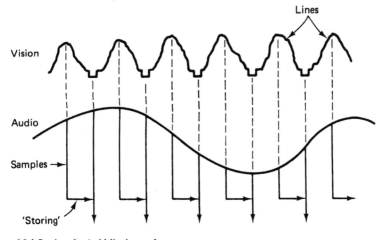

Figure 16.4 Storing the 'mid-line' sample

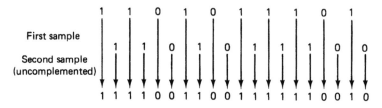

Figure 16.5 Interleaving

variations in the vision signal which follows it, resulting in the picture, or parts of it, being affected. By inverting alternate samples – *complementing* – the mean voltage is kept more constant. Try writing down two similar sets of 1s and 0s, guess at the mean voltage of the interleaved combination and then repeat this with one sample complemented. You should see that the mean voltage doesn't change greatly with complementing, no matter what the proportion of 1s to 0s.

5. Finally the interleaved samples are turned back-to-front. The reason for this is that the most rapid fluctuations in the digital samples will tend to come at the end of the sample and this could cause interference with the start of the vision signal in the next line. By reversing the interleaved set of digits these fluctuations take place at the start when they will be harmless.

SiS is, as we have said, used to carry sound and vision on one circuit to transmitters. There are considerable financial savings in having only one such circuit and the lack of line sync pulses does not matter, except that when there is a need to monitor on the way the SiS information must be stripped out and replaced by proper line syncs, otherwise monitors may not be able to function correctly.

NICAM 728

This is the other NICAM system we referred to and has been developed in the UK for the transmission of stereo television signals. (Mono sound is also transmitted so that compatibility between stereo and mono receivers is maintained. There is, it may be remembered, a similar compatibility requirement in radio.) The number '728' comes from the fact that one complete frame contains 728 bits. Each frame has a duration of 1 millisecond, so the bit-rate is 728 kbits/second. The basic system is similar to the sound-in-syncs that we have just described; the sampling frequency is 32 kHz with an initial resolution of 14 bits, but this is companded, as in the other NICAM method, to ten bits with five ranges. Not all of these 728 bits in each frame are used for the stereo sound – with 32 kHz sampling and ten bits in each sample it follows that 320 bits are

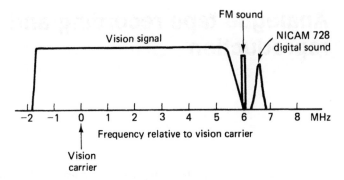

Figure 16.6 Spectrum of a television signal with NICAM 728

needed for each stereo channel, making a total of 640 bits. The remaining bits carry parity, range coding and additional data. The NICAM 728 bits are inserted into the line sync period using a system known as quarternary (i.e. four-level) coding, where each quarternary digit (known as a 'quit') carries the information from two ordinary bits. This doubles the data-carrying capacity. This dual channel signal is thus carried to the transmitters in sound-in-syncs form.

At the transmitter the bit-stream is removed from the video signal, so that the sync pulses are restored to normal, and it is modulated using a system known as *differentially encoded quadrature phase-shift keying* (DQPSK) on to a carrier which is 6.552 MHz above the vision carrier for transmission to receivers. (The apparently peculiar number of 6.552 MHz is exactly nine times 728 kHz). The spectrum of vision and sound is shown in Figure 16.6.

17 Analogue tape recording and reproduction

There are so many aspects of tape recording that, to be reasonably concise, a rather arbitrary starting point has to be chosen. We shall begin with the process of getting analogue signals on to the tape rather than the characteristics of the tape itself. The reasoning behind this is that, in the studio, the tape is an item of equipment whose properties have already been decided before purchase and the engineer/operator has no control over them.

The recording process

The obvious aim in tape recording of any sort is to use what is in effect a small electromagnet (the *record head*) to magnetize the particles on the tape to give as good a replica of the original signal as possible. A direct relationship between magnetic flux and the applied magnetizing force doesn't, however, exist. A high-frequency alternating current has to be mixed with the input audio signal in order to achieve a linear transfer. This high-frequency current is known as *bias*. Its frequency is usually in the region of 100–200 kHz. The exact frequency is not important but the level is rather critical. Figure 17.1 shows the relationship between bias level and other parameters. Thus as the bias current is increased

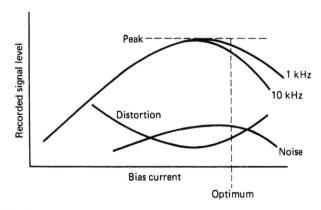

Figure 17.1 Optimum bias setting

there is a steady increase in the recorded signal level, until a maximum is reached. Curiously, this maximum does not coincide with minimum tape noise, so a compromise is adopted, usually taken to be the point where the recorded signal has fallen by 1–3 dB, depending on the frequency. Luckily the stability of the electronics of modern tape machines is such that bias current adjustment usually needs to be done only at intervals, but it should be noted that, strictly, the adjustment ought to be carried out for each different batch of tape. We might mention that there is no easy explanation of why bias works!

Any previous recording on the tape must, of course, be erased. The *erase head* precedes the record head and is fed from the same circuit that provides the bias current, but the erase current is not critical – it is, though, relatively large.

The replay process

Like most things in connection with audio this is not quite as simple as it might appear. Obviously as the tape with recorded signals on it passes the replay head, basically similar in design to the record head, an EMF is induced in the replay head coil. We have, however, a problem. The combination of magnetized tape and replay head is essentially a generator, with the magnets moving rather than the coil. If the frequency of the recorded signal is low then the *rate of change of flux* is low and the induced EMF is small. As the frequency is increased this rate of change of flux also increases and the EMF in the head goes up in proportion. The induced EMF, e, is then proportional to the frequency, f, and doubling the frequency will result in a doubling of e, or a 6 dB increase. There is thus an increase in the output at the rate of 6 dB/octave. This process doesn't, though, go on indefinitely. Figure 17.2 shows a section of the tape passing the gap of a replay head.

The letters N and S represent the North and South poles of a magnetized section of the tape. The distance between two Ns or two Ss is called the *recorded wavelength* and is the magnetic equivalent of a wavelength of the original sound. In the right-hand diagram the head gap happens to be exactly equal to the recorded

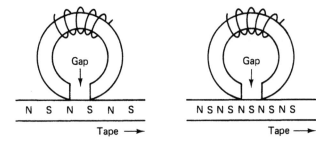

Figure 17.2 Tape passing a replay head

wavelength, so under those conditions there will be no change in the flux and there will be no induced EMF. The frequency at which this occurs is called the *extinction frequency*. We can calculate the extinction frequency from the tape speed and the size of the head gap. Suppose the tape speed is 38 cm/s (0.38 m/s) and the width of the gap is 10 μm (10 × 10⁻⁶ m). To find the extinction frequency we take the recorded wavelength as being equal to the gap width and then:

$$f_{ext} = \frac{0.38 \text{ m/s}}{10 \times 10^{-6} \text{ m}}$$

$$= 38 \text{ kHz}$$

There will, of course, be other extinction frequencies when there are two, three, etc. complete recorded wavelengths in the gap, that is, 76 kHz, 114 kHz and so on, but we are not very concerned about these.

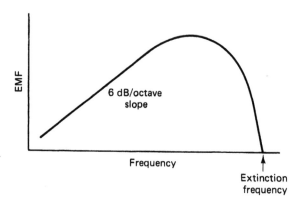

Figure 17.3 Induced EMF in the replay head against frequency

Figure 17.3 shows the EMF induced in the replay head plotted against frequency. Clearly, the useful frequency range is only up to about half the extinction frequency, especially as a simple 6 dB/octave equalizer can correct for the slope up to about this point.

Record and replay equalization

To obtain an overall flat frequency response two types of equalization are used:

1. *Record equalization.* This is a fairly modest correction, being put in to compensate for things like high-frequency losses in the iron of the record head.

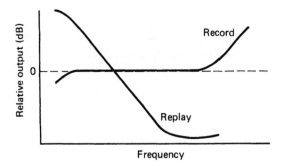

Figure 17.4 Record and replay characteristics

2. *Replay equalization*, which is a much more marked correction. It is a falling curve having a slope of 6 dB/octave until it levels out. This should be a mirror image of the important part of Figure 17.3.

Figure 17.4 shows typical record and equalization characteristics. Note that these characteristics depend on the speed of the tape. On a professional machine there is almost invariably a switch for selecting different tape speeds. Besides changing the speed this switch will also select the appropriate equalization.

Different manufacturers may use one or other of two systems: NAB (National Association of Broadcasters, an American institution) or CCIR (Comité Consultatif International des Radiocommunications, European in origin). Some professional machines have the facility of being switchable from one system to the other.

Azimuth

The term *azimuth* was originally an astronomical one but in recording it has come to mean the angular deviation of a head gap from the vertical. Figure 17.5 illustrates this. Great care has to be taken that there is no azimuth error and on professional machines there are mechanical adjustments to correct it where necessary. Normally the azimuth on a studio machine should not alter but where

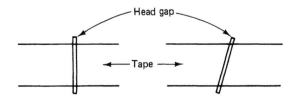

Figure 17.5 Correct and incorrect azimuth

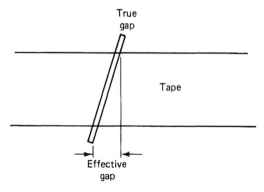

True
gap

Tape

Effective
gap

Figure 17.6 Effects of incorrect azimuth

a machine is mobile, as for example in outside broadcasts (OBs), regular adjustment may be needed. It is good practice also to check the alignment on *any* machine which has had to be transported from one place to another.

The problem which arises from an incorrect adjustment is that the effective head gap is increased (Figure 17.6). On a record head this may not be too serious, but on a replay head the extinction frequency is lowered. In mono recordings this can manifest itself as a loss of high frequencies. On a stereo machine the loss of high frequencies *in stereo listening* may not be apparent – each stereo track is narrow, but the mono signal derived from the stereo may be noticeably lacking in high frequencies.

Full-size professional machines

First a small item of terminology. The heading of this section refers to 'full-size' machines to distinguish reel-to-reel types from cassettes and others. The full-size machines use tape which has a width of 6.25 mm, or a quarter of an inch. It has become a standard item of jargon in the industry to refer to 'quarter-inch' tape and we shall adopt the same term.

Facts about 'quarter-inch' machines

1. The standard tape speed is 38 cm/s (15 ips) but where economy is important and quality can be slightly sacrificed, as in short wave broadcasting, 19 cm/s (7½ ips) is often used.
2. Head gaps are usually in the region of
    (a) *Erase head*. Around 100 μm (0.1 mm). This is large to allow many cycles of the erase current to produce a corresponding number of cycles of flux to

saturate the magnetic particles and then slowly decrease to achieve the demagnetization process.

(b) *Record head.* 20 μm (0.02 mm). This needs to be large enough to allow enough flux to penetrate the magnetic coating.

(c) *Replay head.* 5–10 μm (0.005 mm to 0.01 mm). We have already seen that this needs to be small if the extinction frequency is to be high. Also many machines will operate at 19 cm/s, so a head gap less than our calculated 10 μm is needed.

3. *Multitrack* machines (often 24-track) are large versions of quarter-inch machines. The main and obvious differences apart from the fact that there are many sets of record and replay amplifiers is that the tape is wide – 50 mm, or two inches. A special feature on such machines is the provision of *sync outputs*. These are important when recording tracks which are to be in synchronization with already recorded material. It is necessary for, say, a singer to hear this pre-recorded material but not delayed, as it would be if taken from a replay head. The record heads on the pre-recorded tracks are switched over to be replay heads, thus giving an output in step with what the singer is recording. The quality of the *sync outputs* is generally inferior to that of proper replay heads, because of the greater gap, but the difference is in practice usually very small and in any case, for 'cueing' purposes, is more than adequate.

Some requirements of a professional machine

1. The accuracy of the speed is important, apart from anything else so that timings are meaningful. A maximum of ±0.2% is quoted for high-grade machines. This means a timing error of at most about 3½ seconds in a half-hour recording.
2. The overall frequency response should be within about 2 dB from 30 Hz to 18 kHz and as little as ±1 dB from 60 Hz to about 18 kHz.
3. The start time should be very short – preferably less than 0.5 seconds – so that recorded effects can be played-in without delay and there is generally a prompt and accurate beginning to any replayed material.

Cassette machines

The principles of a cassette machine are exactly the same as in a quarter-inch machine. Originally cassette machines were regarded by the professional world as a joke. They had poor frequency responses, signal-to-noise ratios were abysmal and they were very apt to exhibit *wow* and *flutter* (audible and cyclic speed variations, 'wow' being fairly slow variations and 'flutter' being rapid ones, as the terms suggest). In recent years, however, tape materials have improved, manufacturers have improved the speed control and today, while inevitably inferior to standard tape machines, they are regarded as at least adequate for some purposes in broadcasting. In particular their small size makes them suitable for news reporters in radio to take out. The main drawback is that it is virtually impossible to edit the cassette tape, so that copying to quarter-inch tape, or other editable format, has to be done first.

Facts about cassette machines

1. The tape speed is 4.76 cm/s ($1\frac{7}{8}$ ips) and the tape width is 3.175 mm ($\frac{1}{8}$ inch). There are four tracks in this width, two stereo tracks in each direction, so that each track is roughly 0.75 mm wide. (We shall give more accurate figures later.) Compare this with quarter-inch tape where there are two tracks, each being about 3 mm wide. It is clear that cassette machines will have a much poorer signal-to-noise ratio than quarter-inch machines because of the narrower tracks.
2. With good *noise reduction* systems (see later) the signal-to-noise ratio of a cassette machine can be made to be acceptable.
3. Domestic cassette decks usually have only two heads, one for erase and the other both a record or a replay head, the gap being around 1 μm. Professional machines for static (i.e. studio) use generally have three heads – erase, record and replay. The advantage of this is that 'off-tape monitoring' is possible, the replay head monitoring what has been recorded a fraction of a second earlier (this is a standard feature of quarter-inch machines).
4. A good quality machine will have the following characteristics:
   (a) Frequency response: depends on the tape but around 30 Hz to 20 kHz, ±2.5 dB.
   (b) Signal-to-noise ratio: with noise reduction, up to 70 dB.
   (c) Start time: very short, almost instantaneous.

Cartridge machines

Unlike cassette decks, these have no direct equivalent in the domestic field. They are used in the professional world for jingles and other short sequences, particularly in live programmes. The cartridge itself contains an endless loop of tape, the duration of which can vary from perhaps 30 seconds up to a few minutes. The cartridges are bought with a particular specified duration, rather like cassettes (C30, C90, etc.). The tape is typically 6.5 mm wide and runs at a speed of 19 cm/s ($7\frac{1}{2}$ ips). A cartridge is shown in Figure 17.7.

The tape is taken from the *centre* of the coiled loop and returned to the outside. There is consequently a permanent slip between adjacent turns when the machine is running and specially lubricated tapes have to be used to avoid undue wear.

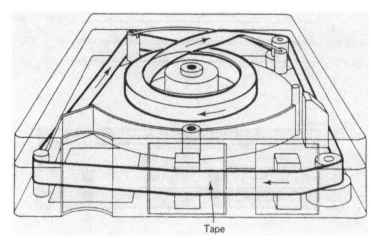

Figure 17.7 Cartridge

Figure 17.8 Cartridge machine

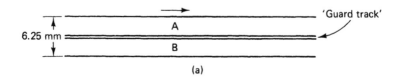

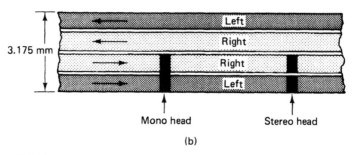

Figure 17.9 (a) Quarter-inch stereo tape; (b) cassette tape

Special tones are automatically put on to a *cue track*. One short tone burst is at the start of the programme sequence and another at the end. When the latter is detected the tape is spooled on until the start tone is found. The tape is then stopped so that it is ready for immediate replay again. A typical high-grade machine is shown in Figure 17.8.

Facts about cartridge machines

1. The start and stop times should be less than 40 ms.
2. A frequency response from 40 Hz to 16 kHz ±1 to 1.5 dB is found on the more modern machines.
3. The signal-to-noise ratio should be better than 50 dB.

Track formats

Quarter-inch and cassette track formats are shown in Figure 17.9.

18 Digital recording and reproduction

Principles of digital tape recording and replay

In some ways recording digits on to tape presents many problems; in other ways it is simpler than analogue recording. Let us take the problems first:

1. Analogue tape can just about cope with the bandwidth 30 Hz to 15 or 16 kHz (about nine octaves). We've already seen that a 16-bit digital signal sampled at 44 kHz is equivalent to more than 700 kbits/s; that's for mono and doesn't include error correction bits! If we said that stereo needs a bandwidth in excess of 2 MHz we shouldn't be far wrong.
2. Magnetic tape, however carefully manufactured, has minute areas where the oxide is thin or even missing. Such patches are called *drop-outs* because in a severe case the audio signal drops in level. With modern high-quality tapes used in analogue recording the effects of a drop-out are almost unknown. At worst there is a slight reduction in level for a fraction of a second. With digital recording a millisecond's worth of drop-out, probably quite undetectable in analogue, could cause the loss of a couple of thousand bits of a digital signal.

When we dealt with error detection we saw the answer to the drop-out problem. The main reason for scatter codes is to counteract the effect of things like drop-outs. The first problem, the high bit-rate, we will deal with more fully a little later.

The ways in which digital tape recording is easier than analogue are:

1. The high frequency of the pulses removes the need for bias.
2. Because the pulses can be severely deformed but still be recognized, and if necessary be regenerated, there is no need for equalization.
3. Slight fluctuations in tape speed, which might cause wow and flutter in an analogue machine, can be 'ironed out' by storing all the pulses for a brief period and then taking them out of the store at the correct rate.

What we have said so far should suggest that the only real difficulty is coping with a very high bit-rate (or large bandwidth, whichever way one likes to think of it).

What, first, are the advantages of digital tape recording? We can list these:

1. A much better signal-to-noise ratio.
2. Multiple copying introduces much less impairment. An analogue signal becomes detectably inferior after only three or four copies. The number of usable copies is far greater (but not infinite) with digital recording.
3. The effect known as *print-through*, where the analogue signal recorded on tape produces a weak but audible copy on adjacent layers of the spool, presents no problem with digital recording because the printed-through digits are too weak to be detected as digits. (Print-through is quite often found on cassettes, especially at the start of the tape, where a faint 'pre-echo' is heard a moment before the music.)
4. The effect of *cross-talk*, which means the accidental pick-up of one track's flux in the head of an adjacent track, doesn't exist, for the same reason that print-through is not a problem.

The main problem, then, is coping with the high bit-rate. There are two recognized ways. The first is to carry out a major redesign of an analogue machine. The second is to adopt the same approach that is used in recording video signals where the problem is similar. The idea is that basically a very high tape speed is needed. Because fast-moving tape is impracticable, a high head-to-tape speed is used: in other words, move the tape *and* the head(s). We will look briefly at both approaches.

Stationary head systems

There are several systems that come under this heading. Most divide the audio signal between a number of tracks, this being equivalent to increasing the tape speed. Individual tracks are very thin and there has to be a special, extremely flexible, tape which 'wraps' easily and accurately round the heads. Also the head gap is small. Methods currently (1995) in use include:

DASH (Digital Audio Stationary Head) and Pro-Digi. The two are not compatible, meaning that tape recorded on one cannot be played on the other, although there are broad similarities between them. Each can handle a large number of tracks – up to 48 in the case of DASH and up to 32 with Pro-Digi; the tape width for two tracks is 6.25 mm (¼ inch), increasing to 25 mm (1 inch) for multitracking (Pro-Digi) and 12 mm (½ inch) DASH.

Editing using a razor blade is possible on the two-track versions, and so that an editor can run the tape slowly to and fro past the replay head to find the edit point there is an analogue track. This is needed because at such slow speeds conversion of the digital signals is not really possible. Loss of data at an edit point is compensated for by error correction systems, in particular the 'scatter' method we referred to in Chapter 15. However, since the data is distributed over a distance on the tape it is impossible for there to be edits closer together than about 4 cm.

Twin-DASH is a system that avoids this problem by having twice the number of tracks so that the signal is recorded twice, but the tape then has to go twice as fast. A small, stationary head system called DCC – Digital Compact Cassette – uses cassettes which are the same size as the familiar audio cassette but have eight digital tracks. To achieve acceptable quality, bearing in mind that the tape speed is only 4.76 cm/s (1⅞ inches/s) there has to be a considerable amount of data reduction and this is achieved using PASC, which we outlined under Data compression in Chapter 16.

A point about DCC machines is that they will play analogue cassettes, but, of course, analogue cassette machines cannot be expected to play DCC cassettes!

DAT

This stands for digital audio tape. The forerunner to the DAT system appeared in the mid 1980s when a Betamax video recorder was connected to a unit providing the ADCs (analogue to digital converters) and DACs (digital to analogue converters). The latter unit not only carried out the conversions but also arranged the digital signals into a form that made the video recorder think that it was still dealing with pictures.

The DAT system has developed from this. It uses a very small cassette, smaller than an analogue audio cassette, and a rotating head as in a video recorder but again much smaller.

There is still the problem of editing. The only possible method is to *dub* (i.e. copy from one machine to another) using techniques that are similar to those used in video editing. On the other hand, DAT machines are relatively inexpensive and they are also small and light.

In the DAT tape format, each helical track contains 196 *blocks* of which 130 are for programme data, the remainder being there to help with the tracking (alignment of the heads with the recorded tracks) and other data. Each of the 130 'programme blocks' contains a 288-bit sequence, illustrated in Figure 18.1.

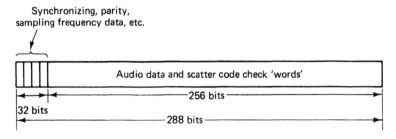

Figure 18.1 The DAT bit sequence

Facts about DAT

There are some differences between various makers' machines, but the following facts are common to all.

1. The cassette dimensions are about 7.4 cm × 5.3 cm × 1.0 cm (an ordinary audio cassette is 10.3 cm × 6.5 cm × 1.0 (min) cm).
2. The tape speed is 8.15 mm/s (47.6 mm/s in an audio cassette).
3. Sampling frequencies are switchable between 48 kHz and 44.1 kHz.
4. 16-bit quantizing is used.
5. The head drum is just under 30 mm diameter and carries two or four heads, depending on the manufacturer.
6. The head drum rotates at 2000 rev/min.
7. The effective dynamic range is >90 dB.
8. Cross-talk between tracks is better than 80 dB.
9. Wow and flutter should be immeasurably low.

Other rotary head digital recording systems include:

DA88 – an 8-track recorder which uses Hi-8 cassettes
Nagra-D – a 4-track open reel recorder using 6.25 mm (¼ inch) tape
ADAT – which uses S-VHS cassettes to give an 8-track machine.

Figure 18.2 A DAT machine

'Hard disk' recording

The so-called 'hard disks' (as opposed to 'floppy disks') used in very many computers have found an important niche in digital recording. Their use is currently increasing and their large storage capacity and extremely rapid access times – meaning that a recorded section can be located very quickly indeed – are useful attributes.

The future of tape recording?

This is pure speculation but it may well be that the days of moving tape are limited. Much of the complexity, and hence cost, of any recording system, whether analogue or digital, is in arranging for there to be relative movement between the tape and the head or heads at the correct speed and alignment. It seems likely that the next major step will be to have solid-state storage. Indeed this exists in some applications but the duration of any stored audio signals in solid state is currently rather short. With the development of bigger memory chips – non-volatile, of course – capable of holding at least 60 minutes' worth of high quality stereo, compact recording devices could become feasible. Without any motors the power consumption could be very small – an important point in portable equipment. Editing could be totally non-destructive; presumably the process of, say, removing a word would be a matter of keying-in data about the start and finish times of the word and then this section would either be removed to another part of the memory or, more probably, would be skipped when 'replaying'. At present (1995) totally solid state recorders are just beginning to appear. The next few years are going to be interesting!

Compact discs

Compact discs (CDs) are, like 'old-fashioned' gramophone records (now generally referred to as vinyl discs), replay-only devices. The digital signals, of which we shall give some details later, are impressed using a laser as a series of tiny 'pits' in a spiral groove. The steps in the process of making a CD are:

1. The laser whose beam is modulated by the digital signals strikes a photo-sensitive material on a glass plate.
2. This material is developed and etched to produce a usable set of pits. It is next silver-plated.
3. The silver-plating is electroplated with nickel to form a reasonably rugged layer. This layer, the 'father', is peeled off the original (the 'master') and is thus a reversal of the master's surface.

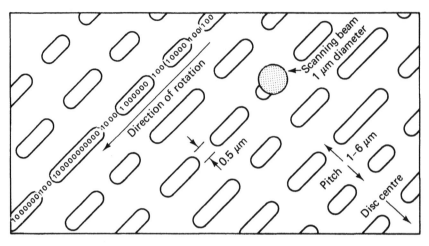

Figure 18.3 Surface of a compact disc

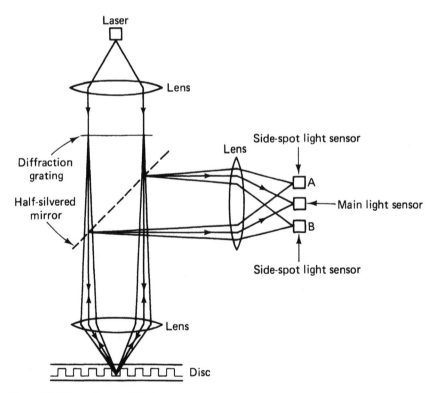

Figure 18.4 The optics of a CD player

4. The father is used to make further versions, ending up with a number of replicas which can be used to produce the actual CD by injection moulding on a glass plate. These last versions are coated with aluminium to make them light reflecting, and they are finally given a layer of protective resin.

Figure 18.3 shows the much-magnified surface of a disc.

The next stage is the replay process, where again a laser is used. The optics of this process can be rather complicated. The basics are shown in Figure 18.4.

The point about using a laser is that this is the only way of focusing a light beam with sufficient accuracy. Ordinary 'white' light is a mixture of wavelengths, and because a lens has a different action on each wavelength it means that really accurate focusing is impossible. Manufacturers of high-grade camera lenses manage to reduce these aberrations to a minimum but a laser, whose beam is truly monochromatic (one wavelength), gives a much better result besides being more compact, lighter and maybe even cheaper.

As Figure 18.4 shows, the laser beam is split into three to allow accurate tracking of the spiral of pits, a process we shall explain shortly.

An important point is worth making here. The bottom of the pits may not reflect an accurate beam into the detector so the digital pattern on the disc's surface is so designed that it is the *changes* in the bit-stream which are significant.

The laser beam is wide at the disc surface, coming to a sharp focus on the track. This means that minor surface blemishes are out of focus and thus not likely to be detected.

Tracking, the process of making sure that the laser beam follows the correct track, makes use of the three-way split in the beam. Figure 18.5 helps to explain

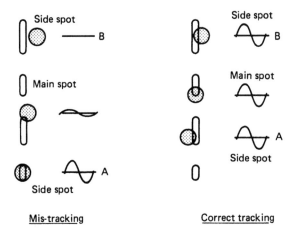

Mis-tracking   Correct tracking

Figure 18.5 The tracking process on a CD

this. If, in Figure 18.5, the laser beam drifts to one side of the centre line then a larger signal is picked up in photo-detector A than in B. The difference constitutes an *error signal* which can be used to bring the laser back into its correct position.

Facts about CD players

1. The spiral track starts at the *centre* of the disc.
2. To keep a constant track speed under the laser the rate of rotation of the disc varies from about 500 rev/min at the centre to about 200 rev/min at the outside.
3. Complex error-correction methods are used. In theory a hole some 2 mm diameter could be drilled through the playing surface without being audible. (You are advised not to try this on any valued CD.)
4. Although the CD system is theoretically immune to the effects of surface contamination it is advisable to handle CDs with reasonable care.
5. The scanning speed is around 1.2 m/s. Taking a playing time of 60 minutes plus around 20 minutes worth of error correction gives an approximate track length of nearly 6 km!
6. General performance figures can be summarized by:
   Frequency response: 20 Hz–20 kHz ± 0.5 dB
   Signal-to-noise ratio: 90 dB

Recordable CDs

For many years after CDs were introduced they were regarded, rightly, as things that could be bought but could not be produced except by major manufacturing organizations! Things change, though, and modest size, reasonable cost units are now to be found in many studio environments. The 'CDR' – Recordable CD – looks very similar to a conventional one. It is a record-once disc, meaning that the data on it cannot be erased, and the recording is made by a laser altering the characteristics of a special dye. There is a resulting change in the colour of the recording surface and this is equivalent to the pattern of pits on a normal CD. CDRs can be played on an ordinary CD machine.

Magneto Optical discs

Again a laser is used to make the recording, this time to heat a special plastic layer inside a glass disc when a magnetic field is applied. In replay a low-power laser is focused on the track and an ingenious use of polarizing filters allows the the data to be read. MO discs have the advantage of being re-recordable.

Oversampling

This term often appears on digital equipment and it is as well to state briefly what it means. Given a sampling frequency of, say, 44 kHz it is possible for there to be *intermodulation* products – that is, spurious frequencies arising from the interaction between 44 kHz and harmonics of the audio frequencies. To separate out these unwanted signals requires very sharp filters (*'brick-wall' filters*) which are difficult to design and/or expensive. The trick is to introduce at the decoding end what is in effect a process which operates as though the sampling frequency were higher than the original. This is known as *oversampling*. Thus, 'two-times oversampling' means decoding as though the sampling frequency had been 88 kHz. This moves the intermodulation products to much higher frequencies, which can then be more easily filtered. 'Four times oversampling' pretends that the sampling frequency had been 1760 kHz.

19   Noise reduction (analogue)

It has been the practice so far in this book to avoid references to specific types of equipment on the grounds that we're concerned with the principles behind the technology and not the details, which may vary greatly from one piece of equipment to another. However, when it comes to noise reduction we cannot get away from dealing with particular systems. There are not all that many successful ones, and their names have tended to creep into the terminology. (Those of us who are concerned about the purity of the English language may wince at the verb 'to Dolby', or even worse 'to de-Dolby', but there are no easy alternatives without being pedantic.) So we shall deal with the specific systems in turn.

We've made many references to noise and signal-to-noise ratios and have made the point that noise is always with us, either resulting from the movement of electrons or because, in recording, we are ultimately dealing with particles of magnetic material which can never be infinitely small. We've seen that the use of digital technology can go a very long way towards eliminating the effects of noise, but analogue processes will be with us for a long time yet and it is here that methods of reducing the inherent system noise can be very useful. The various professional noise reduction systems work basically by reducing the dynamic range before entering the noisy domain (the analogue tape, for example) and expanding it afterwards – using a *compander* in fact, which is a *com*pressor followed by an ex*pander*.

Dolby A

The Dolby A system is widely used in analogue recording, especially multitrack work, where the tape noise may be reduced by about 10–15 dB. It is also employed in long-distance analogue links but its use there has diminished with increasing use of digital links via satellites. The system avoids many of the undesirable effects which a simple compander can introduce. We will list these possible ill effects and show how the Dolby A system avoids, or at least greatly minimizes, them.

1. It isn't easy to make a compressor/expander *track* accurately – that is, expand the dynamic range by exactly the same amount by which it has been reduced.

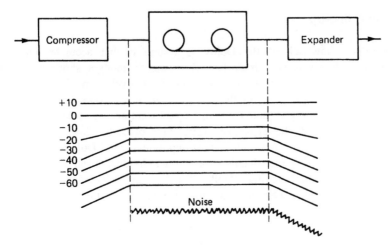

Figure 19.1 Dolby A action on the low signal levels

The Dolby system uses the same circuitry for both processes since it works by subtracting or adding as appropriate a portion of the audio signal. It is thus a linear process.

2. A compander works on the higher levels of the audio signal, as we saw when dealing with limiters and compressors. But the higher levels are those which will tend to mask the noise and therefore are those parts which need noise reduction least of all. The Dolby A system detects when the signal levels are low and raises these at compression and lowers them again in expansion. The low levels are in a way 'lifted over' the noise, as in Figure 19.1.

3. Companding action over the entire frequency range may result in unwanted modulation effects. Thus, if a high-level signal and a low-level one occur at widely different frequencies the processing will take place because of the low-level one, although the other does not need any action. To avoid this the Dolby A system divides the frequency range into four bands, each designed to help defeat particular types of noise. See Table 19.1.

Table 19.1 Frequency range bands

Band	Frequency range	Type of noise targeted
I	Below 80 Hz	Hum and rumble
II	80 Hz to 3 kHz	Cross-talk and print-through
III	3 kHz and above	Hiss and modulation noise
IV	9 kHz and above	Hiss and modulation noise

Dolby A line-up

One minor drawback of the Dolby A system is that accurate line-up of programme levels is very important. A moment's thought shows that if the *encoder* introduces compression because the signal level is low then the *decoder* must receive the signals at exactly the right level if it is to expand correctly. If, say, the already Dolbyed (note the verb!) signal went into the decoder at a higher level than intended, the expansion would take place too low in the signal's dynamic range. For this reason it is most important that all Dolby-encoded tapes are clearly marked. Exact details depend on individual installations, but it is worth pointing out here that 'Dolby Tone' – an easily identifiable warble produced by frequency changing, not level changing – must always be put on the start of any tape. This does two things: it identifies for later operators that the tape is Dolby encoded and it also helps the signal levels to be correctly set. The Dolby units themselves contain the circuitry for producing the tone.

Dolby B

The Dolby A system is relatively expensive, although not a large proportion of the cost of a professional tape machine. For example, the cost of 24 Dolby units, although considerable, is still small compared with the cost of a 24-track machine.

The Dolby B system is a low-cost version designed to be used with cassette players where the tape noise, unless treated, is objectionable. It was originally intended for the domestic market, as indeed were cassettes, but it is now being used professionally not only with audio cassettes but also with the sound tracks of various types of video equipment.

Dolby B is a much simplified version of Dolby A, the principle of operation being exactly similar but using only one frequency band, namely from 2 kHz to 5 kHz and above. The lower frequency of the band is variable. (Notice that tape noise – 'hiss' – is predominantly a high frequency effect and falls largely into the band dealt with by Dolby B.) All pre-recorded audio cassettes (unless they are very old, say from the early 1960s) are Dolby B encoded.

Dolby C

Dolby C is a later and improved version of Dolby B, again intended for audio cassettes. It has two frequency bands, and in that sense is nearer to the A system. Most good quality cassette decks incorporate Dolby C as well as B. About 20 dB of noise reduction can be obtained.

Dolby SR ('spectral recording')

The latest of the Dolby systems (it appeared first in 1986), Dolby SR embodies concepts from the A, B and C systems. The word 'spectral' refers to the spectrum of the audio range which is analysed in the processing.

To see how Dolby SR works we need to look at its action at low signal levels, medium levels and high levels.

1. *Low levels*. The idea here is to use a high recording level using a fixed equalization.
2. *Medium levels*. With an increase in signal level there could be a risk of overload so some gain reduction is applied. Basically there is a group of variable filters. Some are of variable bandwidth and some are of variable gain. The fixed-bandwidth ones have their gain electronically varied, while those with fixed gain are adjusted to cover different frequency ranges. A control circuit thus creates in effect a very large number of filters which are appropriate to the programme signal.
3. *High levels*. Gain reduction takes place, but only in the frequency region near to that of the high level signal.

Overall a noise reduction of up to 24 dB can be obtained with Dolby SR. This makes analogue recordings have noise figures comparable with digital recordings, but beware: the comparison mustn't be taken too far. To equate SR recordings with digital neglects the fact that with multiple copying, SR recordings, as with any other analogue recordings, will deteriorate after relatively few copies.

dbx

This is a relatively straightforward compander system, using a 2:1 compressor and matching expander. The use of *pre-emphasis*, that is high frequency lift in recording which is subsequently corrected in replay, improves the performance by causing more compression at the high frequencies. Additional signals outside the audio band are used to match the expander to the compressor. One advantage is that line-up of levels is not critical and the noise reduction figures are impressive – around 25–30 dB is quoted. However, it is possible for the companding process to be audible and also the effects of tape drop-outs are magnified by 2:1 on replay.

Telecom c4

Telecom c4 is relatively little used in the UK; it is more popular in other parts of Europe. It can be thought of as a combination of Dolby A and dbx in that four frequency bands are used (like Dolby A) and a compander system is employed as in dbx, one compander to each band. However, the companding is carried out at 1:1.5, not 1:2 – the lower the ratio the better in the interests of minimizing processing. The four frequency bands are:

I   up to 215 Hz
II   215 Hz to 1.45 kHz
III   1.45 kHz to 4.8 kHz
IV   4.8 kHz and above

Disadvantages of Telecom c4 are that, as with dbx, things like tape drop-outs are magnified in the expansion process and it is also the most costly system. Noise reduction of 15 dB or more can be obtained.

20 Public address

Except for some musical programmes, a studio audience almost always needs loudspeaker reinforcement of the programme sound, a point we made when dealing with sound desks. And as we said there, the term 'sound reinforcement' would be the more accurate term to use. But like it or not the term PA has come to be the accepted one, rather like the use of 'echo' when we should say 'artificial reverberation'.

Public address or sound reinforcement?

It isn't always realized that there is, or should be, a big difference between the two. Strictly we ought to use the term 'public address' (PA) when a large number of people are being spoken to via loudspeakers, as, for example, in commentaries at a race meeting. Sound reinforcement, on the other hand, means exactly what it says – the audience can hear something directly but loudspeakers are needed for complete audibility. There is, of course, a grey area where sound reinforcement merges into PA but that need not concern us.

In terms of the technology probably the best distinction to draw is based on whether or not the microphones can pick up the output of the loudspeakers. If they can't it's PA; if they can it's sound reinforcement. And if they can there is generally a major problem–*howlround*. Everyone has experienced the embarrassing squeal, shriek or whistle which is the oscillation caused by a microphone picking up its own output from a loudspeaker. The effect is sometimes called 'feedback', but this word can be applied to very many situations, in many cases deliberate and beneficial, when a signal is returned to an earlier stage. Here we will use the more descriptive word 'howlround'.

Requirements of PA

We are dealing here with a rather specialized aspect of PA – namely reinforcement for the benefit of a studio audience. PA at a rock concert is a rather different matter, although there are some basic similarities. The needs for a studio PA system are:

1. The audience should be able to hear clearly an appropriate version of the studio's output.
2. There should not be any regions where the PA level is either too loud or too quiet.
3. The output of the studio microphones should not normally be coloured by the PA. (We say 'normally' because there are sometimes situations where the suggestion of PA in the background can help to convey atmosphere to the listeners.)
4. There must be no howlrounds.

The problem of howlround

The mechanism of a howlround is slightly more complicated than might appear. Figure 20.1 represents the basic situation. The microphone, its amplifier, the 'room' and the loudspeaker form a loop. The room can be thought of as an attenuator simply because of the reduction in sound wave intensity from loudspeaker to microphone. If the overall gain in the loop is less than unity then

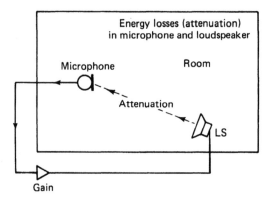

Figure 20.1 A 'PA' situation

the signal energy will die away. If, though, it is *greater* than unity then oscillation is very likely to occur. It would seem a simple matter to make sure that the amplifier gain was set so that the loop gain never exceeded unity, but this is complicated by the frequency responses of the components of the loop. Figure 20.2 shows why.

The uppermost frequency response curve is typical of many rooms (studios, halls, and so on). It is uneven because of things like standing waves and it may vary from the mean by ±10 dB or possibly more. The flattest response graph is probably going to be that of the microphone, which we have shown here as

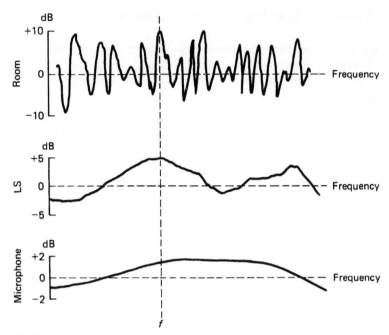

Figure 20.2 Frequency responses within the PA loop

fluctuating by ±2 dB – in practice the microphone's response might be better or worse than that.

We have shown the response of the loudspeaker as varying by ±5 dB. Again this is an arbitrarily chosen figure but is what one might expect from many PA loudspeakers. The actual figures don't in fact matter very much as far as we are concerned here. The point is that at some frequency, f in the diagram, the combined responses of room, loudspeaker and microphone result in several decibels of extra gain. In our illustration it could be around 12–15 dB. This means that at f the loop gain is much higher than the mean gain, and it is at this frequency that a howl will occur first. Note that moving the microphone, probably the most portable part of the loop, will probably result in a change of the howl frequency because the room response refers to one and only one acoustic path.

We will look at ways of minimizing the risk of howlround, because until that battle has been won there is probably little hope of achieving satisfactory PA for an audience. There are in principle several techniques which can be useful but in practice some of these are not easily available. For example, we shall mention the siting of loudspeakers, but in many situations these are firmly fixed in position in the studio and cannot easily be moved. In outside broadcasts, for example, the realistic sites are often very few, sometimes because of local regulations dealing with safety for audiences.

The choice and siting of loudspeakers

The line-source speakers we referred to in Chapter 9 are obvious candidates. Their directional properties mean that microphones can, in theory, be placed in the relatively dead regions. As we pointed out earlier, the quality of very many such loudspeakers is not particularly good – perfectly adequate for speech but barely good enough for music. Contrary to expectation, good quality conventional loudspeakers *can* be used for PA; there is a greater risk of howlround of course, but sometimes the risk is not as great as one might expect, due maybe to the flatter frequency response of the quality loudspeaker.

In the matter of positioning loudspeakers it's obvious that where possible line-source speakers should, if at all possible, be mounted with the microphone(s) on their dead axes. This is not always possible, of course. If the loudspeakers are some distance from the microphone area then their angling may be less important as reflections and reverberation generally will cause the sound to be diffuse.

Choice of microphones

Cardioids or hypercardioids with their dead sides directed at the loudspeakers are other obvious choices. However, depending on circumstances, it is possible for there still to be problems. Sound may be reflected on to the microphone's live side. This is especially likely in radio outside broadcasts from places such as school halls. Small personal microphones, although usually omnidirectional, don't usually seem to be as bad as one might expect. It may be that the body of the wearer has a screening effect.

Electrical processing of the audio signal

There are two methods which have had varying degrees of popularity. The first is the use of *frequency shifters* – units which change the audio frequencies by a few hertz. These units seem to go in and out of fashion with some regularity. The basic theory is good. It is based on the observation made in the 1950s or possibly earlier that the peaks in a room's response (see the upper graph in Figure 20.2) are on average spaced by approximately $(4/RT)$ Hz, RT being of course, the reverberation time. If the RT were, say, 2 s then the peaks would, statistically, be spaced by about 2 Hz. If the frequency of the PA feed is shifted by half this, 1 Hz in our example, then the peaks striking the microphone will be moved to coincide with troughs, and so on, with the result that the room response is in effect flattened. It doesn't work quite like this, though. To begin with, the relationship between peak spacing and RT is only true *on average*, but it is quite possible to get up to about 6 dB of PA 'stability' that is, either 6 dB more PA level or a 6 dB safety margin.

The trouble with PA shifters is that if there is a howl it is likely to be a weird rising or falling oscillation which is far worse than a plain howlround. Also it is disastrous if a singer hears any of the shifted PA – he or she finds this very disturbing to sing against. In general many (but not necessarily all) operators have found that frequency shifting is not a good way of coping with the problem.

The second method simply introduces equalization. A graphic equalizer can be set up by ear to 'tune-out' incipient howls. Expensive frequency analysers are sometimes used to find the peaks in the loop but they are often not worth the cost and time taken. It doesn't take much practice to find the right filter by trial and error. It's tempting to think that a ⅓-octave equalizer will be best as the filters are very sharp and can be used to remove narrow peaks. This is sometimes true, but extensive use of a ⅓-octave unit can wreak such havoc with the frequency response of the PA feed that the quality is much impaired. There are many cases when an octave equalizer is very adequate, as well as being much easier to set up.

The PA mixer

This means a person and not a piece of equipment! A very good way of giving a studio audience a respectable sound reinforcement is to have an experienced operator with a small sound mixing desk actually in the audience. This desk can be fed with selected outputs from the main desk – possibly *group outputs* – and the operator can balance these and guard against incipient howls at the same time. The only drawbacks are that an extra skilled operator is needed and there must be a small sound desk available and space to put it. These are generally impossible requirements in outside broadcasts but are feasible as fixed installations in a broadcasting studio, which is used very largely for programmes with an audience.

Finally, as with so much else when one is dealing with sound waves, good PA is often a matter of trial and error, but an understanding of the principles can greatly reduce the proportion of error.

21   More uses of digits

Reverberation or echo?

To get the terminology right, remember that with *echo* there is a perceptible time difference between hearing the direct sound and the reflection. This time difference is fairly critical. If it is more than about 40 ms the brain is aware of the gap. Less than this and the gap is not noticed *as an audible delay* but the brain may nevertheless register unconsciously that a time difference has occurred. Delays of only a few milliseconds are associated with small rooms – longer ones, say 20 ms or so, are recognized as being appropriate to large enclosures.

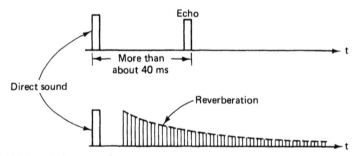

Figure 21.1 Echo and reverberation

Reverberation, on the other hand, means the decay of sound resulting from multiple reflections. It is ideally a continuous process and we explained it in Chapter 6. But, as we've seen, the word 'echo' gets used to mean reverberation, so to conform with a dubious practice, we shall use it from time to time.

Artificial reverberation

Under the heading of sound desks we looked at methods of handling the 'echo' signal but we avoided anything more than a passing reference to the devices used to create a reverberant effect. Many ingenious methods have been used in the past:

1. *Echo chambers* (echo rooms). These are as large as possible with acoustically reflective surfaces and containing a loudspeaker emitting the *direct* sound with one or two microphones picking up the reverberated version of the direct signal. Such rooms can be very realistic in their effect, but it isn't easy to vary the RT and the rooms are very wasteful of precious space.
2. *Tape loop devices*. A continuous loop of tape has the direct signal recorded on it and a number of replay heads give the effect of multiple reflections. They usually sounded like some sort of flutter effect, which could be useful sometimes but wasn't really reverberation.
3. *Springs*. One or more helical springs had moving coil transducers fed with the direct signal to set the spring(s) into vibration. Further transducer(s) picked up the reverberating output. At best these worked well and gave a realistic reverberation effect. At worst they were rather 'twangy'.
4. *The echo plate*. A sheet of steel, usually $2\,m \times 1\,m$, was set into vibration by a transducer near the centre, thus producing ripples in the steel. Other transducers picked up the vibrations. The plate was, in effect, a two-dimensional room, the edges taking the place of walls and it was possible to alter the RT by moving an absorbent plate nearer to or further from the steel plate. Good plates could be very good, others could give a rather 'tinny' effect.

These devices worked – some really very well, while others were only just satisfactory. If they were good, they tended to be both large and expensive; in their heyday at the end of the 1960s or early 1970s costs were of the order of £2000. (The reader can scale that up to present-day values.) The advent of good *digital* reverberators has changed the picture entirely.

The detailed operation of a digital reverberation unit is too complex to go into here. It must be enough to say that the direct signal goes into an ADC (analogue-to-digital converter) using typically a 16-bit system and 44k Hz sampling. A store, a better term for which is *tapped delay line*, holds the digitized signal which is suitably filtered and returned, under the control of a microprocessor, to the input of the store to maintain a long reverberation time. Other filters carry out further tasks to include, for example, varying the phase of components of the signal, an effect which occurs in real-life reverberation. Besides varying the reverberation time a number of programs are normally available within the device and selectable from controls on the front panel or on a remote control unit. These may, for example, give the effect of changing the room size. One way of doing this is to vary the *initial time delay* (ITD) which, as we saw at the beginning of this chapter, is important to the brain in assessing the apparent size of a room. Also a form of 'equalization' is used to vary the RT with frequency; we found in the chapters dealing with room acoustics that the air provides absorption at high frequencies and this becomes noticeable with large enclosures.

All in all a modern digital reverberation unit can simulate, usually very successfully, a wide range of acoustic conditions and at a cost which is usually very much less than that of the electromechanical devices such as springs and plates. In fact some digital reverberation devices, albeit with restricted facilities, can provide excellent reverberation simulations at a cost which is comparable with, say, a good domestic cassette deck.

Digital delay

We've already mentioned one use of a delay system – in artifical reverberation units. There is, though, a big part to be played by a straight delay and there are many commercially available units which can delay an audio signal by amounts varying from 1 ms to a second or two. Most use 44 kHz sampling and operate with 16-bit resolution. In many the output can be fed back to the input to provide a 'flutter' effect. Typical uses are:

1. To provide a special sound effect in pop music, or to create 'space' sounds in drama.
2. *Automatic double tracking* (ADT), making a vocalist sing a duet with him or herself. The basic signal from the singer's microphone is split in the sound desk and one feed may be panned to one side of the stereo image. The other feed is delayed slightly – only a few milliseconds – and panned to the other side. This can give the effect of two singers. As we have described it the effect is not very satisfactory – to begin with the mono version may sound very odd, especially at frequencies whose period coincides with the delay period – and better effects result if there is also a slight *pitch change* (see below) and also a small fluctuation in the delay.
3. *'Flanging'*. A curious effect, very difficult to describe, results if part of a signal is delayed slightly and then mixed with the original. The term is said to have originated in the days of the Beatles when someone noticed that if two tape machines were operating in step and then the flange of one of the spools was slowed slightly by resting a finger lightly on the edge then this effect resulted. It is another of the audio 'special effects' which finds a place in things like drama, pop music and certain sounds intended to create an 'unearthly' effect.

Pitch change

This is a special version of delay. If a digitized audio signal is fed into a store and then taken out of that store at a different rate the final analogue signal is changed in pitch. Figure 21.2 is a simplified representation of this. Suppose that A, B, C, D, ... are stores, each holding one sample. The figure shows only a few; in practice there must be a very large number. The arrow marked IN can be thought of as an electronic switch rotating clockwise and putting successive samples into

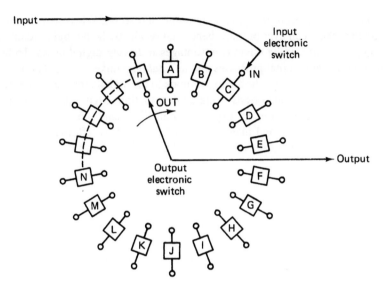

Figure 21.2 Explaining pitch change

each store in turn. The second arrow, OUT, is a second electronic switch which reads the contents of each store. (There must also be an arrangement to empty each store after it has been read.) If the OUT arrow rotates at the same speed as the IN arrow then there is simply a delay between the input and the output signals. If, however, the OUT arrow rotates slower than the IN arrow the output signal will be reproduced at a lower pitch; if it rotates faster the pitch is raised.

The perceptive reader will immediately be wondering what happens when the arrows catch up with each other. In short there is a problem! If the OUT catches up with the IN it may find the stores are all empty; if the OUT is caught up with by the IN the stores are already full and have been read once already. The solution is for the system to repeat samples or jump samples as appropriate. There is likely to be a small audible effect, called a *glitch*. In early pitch changers this was likely to be disturbing unless the pitch change was very small, 1% or 2%, so that the glitches occurred relatively infrequently. More modern devices have clever arrangements which make the glitches much more inconspicuous. One trick, for example, is to repeat or jump samples only when the audio signal is at a very low level – ideally zero when a repeat or a jump would have no effect.

Digital sound desks (digital mixing)

The ideal, but not yet achieved, signal path from microphone to listener's loudspeaker must surely be a purely digital one. We have looked at digital recording, transmission, delay, reverberation, and so on. Whether microphones and loudspeakers can ever produce beneficial results by being digital remains to be seen, but there can be obvious advantages in having digital desks. To begin with, having many digital processes and an *analogue* mixer means that there are frequent conversions from the analogue mode to the digital mode and back again. This is expensive and also leads to signal degradation. Digital desks, when they first appeared, were extremely expensive but, like many other digital devices, their prices have fallen and many can now be classed as 'affordable'. Here we can do no more than outline a very few of the problems and their solutions.

Digital faders

In analogue desks the fader is simply a resistive device which 'weakens' the audio signal. Putting such a fader into a digital bit-stream will simply lower the amplitude of the pulses and this will have no effect until the pulse amplitudes are too small to be identified, when the signal will cease. It would be an expensive, and probably noisy, switch.

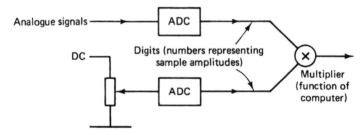

Figure 21.3 A simplified digital fader

To take a simple example of the function of a digital fader, to reduce the level of an analogue signal by 6 dB means halving the voltage. Thinking in digital terms this means *dividing the number which represents the sample amplitude by 2.* In other words any fading or attenuating process involves arithmetical operations. Figure 21.3 gives a simple illustration. The processing speed has to be very high. The calculations must be carried out at the sampling frequency so we are talking about 44 000 or 48 000 such operations a second.

Mixing

In an analogue desk channels and groups, for example, are combined by simply putting the various signals on to a busbar. A similar operation with digital signals

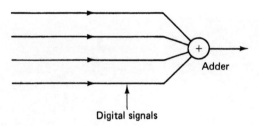

Figure 21.4 Digital mixing

would result in a meaningless jumble of pulses. The only way of performing such a process with digital signals is to *add* the numbers representing the samples, as in Figure 21.4.

Filters (EQ)

This is much too complicated a process to try to explain here. It must be sufficient simply to state that if successive samples are delayed and then added after a multiplying process it is possible to produce the equivalent of EQ. Control settings of, say, the amount of 'top lift' alter the multiplying factors linked to each store.

Compression

We'll leave it to you to try to visualize what digital processes are involved. A compressor is, after all, a form of automatic fader.

Sampling

This is not to be confused with the sampling of an audio signal that is the first stage of conversion from analogue to digital. Here we mean taking an appreciable chunk, up to a few seconds, of a signal and storing it. Once stored the digital stream can be manipulated by, for example, adjusting the start or finish points. The important thing is that this is non-destructive. In other words, if a particular syllable of a word is to be processed the entire word, or even phrase containing that word, is stored and the start and end points of the wanted part can be found by trial and error. Nothing of the stored sample is destroyed, or at least not until the operator chooses to do so. Very precise selection of a wanted effect is thus possible.

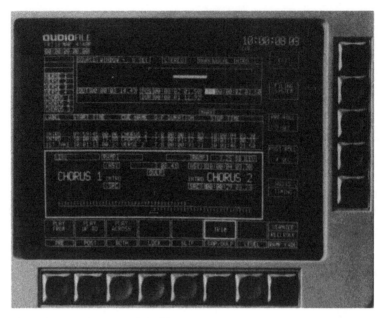

Figure 21.5 Screen display of a digital editing system

Digital editing

In a sense this is sampling on a big scale. It finds wide application in radio and television post-dubbing operations, where sound effects have to be added very accurately to pre-recorded dialogue and, in television, accompanying pictures. The various audio signals to be handled are recorded in digital form on a hard disc which not only has a large capacity but also offers very rapid retrieval. Start and finish points can be selected and edits carried out, again without damaging the original. Thus if an edit is found not to be quite right it can be repeated many times until it is, unlike analogue tape editing where a razor blade is used and it can be difficult or even impossible to change the editing point. To make things easier for the editor there is often a full screen display. In one system, for instance, part of the display shows a representation of a moving tape with a tape replay head. Although the equipment is fully digital such a display helps the operator to visualize what is happening in analogue terms. Figure 21.5 shows one of the screen displays in a widely-used digital editor.

Time code

At the end of the 1960s there came a need for providing synchronization for videotape machines, basically to allow editing of pictures to take place. The

Society of Motion Picture and Television Engineers (SMPTE) in the United States developed a digital code which fulfilled the need of giving precise timing information. This code was adopted in Europe by the EBU (European Broadcasting Union) and is correctly termed the *SMPTE/EBU Time Code*. More commonly it's called just the SMPTE time code, and usually pronounced 'simpty'. The reason for including time code in a book about sound technology is that the SMPTE time code is widely used for synchronizing sound tape machines either with each other or with videotape machines. Indeed in computer-assisted mixing time code is vital for letting the computer know the current position of the tape in the multitrack machine.

Time code (unless told the contrary you can assume this to mean the SMPTE code) consists of an 80-bit digital signal which carries information about HOURS, MINUTES, SECONDS and FRAMES; in the UK and most of Europe a frame is $\frac{1}{25}$ second. The arrangement of the 80 bits is:

bits 0–3 and 8–9   frame count
bits 16–19 and 24–26   seconds
bits 32–36 and 40–44   minutes
bits 48–52 and 56–60   hours

There is also a set of 12 bits (64–80) which is called the *sync word*. This marks the end of a complete sequence and also gives information about the direction of travel of the tape. Besides one or two extra bits for extra information there are four groups of eight bits called the *user bits*. These 32 bits are 'spares' which can be made to carry extra information chosen by, naturally, the user.

The code is put on to, for example, a 24-track tape, using a *time code generator* which may be incorporated into the equipment or may be a separate unit. Usually, in audio operations, the time code is started at zero time; in television recordings the time code could be the time of day.

To synchronize two tapes (and we will think of audio tapes) there has to be a *synchronizer* which compares the time code readings from the two machines. If there is a difference then a control signal is fed into one of the machines to speed it up or slow it down until the readings are the same.

We've talked about the use of time code in synchronizing two (or more) machines. While this is perfectly valid the use of time code doesn't only mean making these machines run in step with each other. For example, a sound or video recording carrying time code can be 'marked' very accurately by noting the time code reading where an edit is to be made. This may be done by simply pressing a button, and if this point is found to be inaccurate the synchronizer can be instructed to 'offset' the edit point by any number of frames. If time code is fed into a loudspeaker the resulting buzz is very unpleasant. To minimize the risk of this happening, even as a consequence of cross-talk from one tape track to another, time code is usually put on to an outside track (if it is a 24-track tape this is generally number 24), if possible leaving track 23 blank. The time code track is then well isolated from all audio tracks. (The cross-talk problem is generally less serious with modern tape machines than it was with earlier ones.)

MIDI (musical instrument digital interface)

This is an internationally agreed standard which allows electronic musical instruments, computers, synthesizers and so on to be connected together in such a way that operating or playing one device triggers the others to produce their versions of the same note. Very many electronic instruments have MIDI connections at their back and these take the form of 5-pin DIN sockets, usually marked IN, OUT and THRU, the latter allowing MIDI units to be 'daisy-chained' together.

A complete explanation of MIDI would be far too long to go into here, but we can give an outline.

To begin with there is no unique device called MIDI. MIDI simply defines a standard which manufacturers can adopt. In a sense, then, it's a little like time code. Exactly *how* a manufacturer meets the MIDI specification is up to him. Incidentally the full specification runs to a medium-sized book.

The interfacing cable which links one MIDI device to another carries the digital data about an originating sound signal at a rate of about 31 kbits/second. This high rate is necessary if sufficient information about a note is to be handled rapidly enough for there to be no serious delays.

One important characteristic of MIDI is that there are 16 *channels*. These are not the same kind of channel as in a sound desk. In MIDI terms a channel is part of a time-division multiplexed message route which may be directed to one or more other instruments. Thus each instrument may be assigned to a specific channel. A typical channel message could contain, amongst other things, data which trigger a slave instrument to play a note which could be its own version of an original sound, or start a sequence which is synchronized with the original but is otherwise perhaps quite different. The channel data can include, for instance:

● start and finish times of a note,
● pitch of the original note,
● velocity with which the original key was struck,
● characteristics of any 'pitch bender' (i.e. pitch change).

There are four *channel assignments*. This may be set on an instrument to decide what channels it will respond to. The four are:

1. OMNI ON (i.e. *all* on). The instrument responds to all messages it receives, regardless of channel.

2. OMNI OFF (the opposite of *all* on). The instrument is assigned to one channel only. This means it will respond to messages on that channel only and will normally transmit on the same channel.
3. POLY (short for *polyphonically*). This means that there is the capability of more than one note for each channel – in other words, chords.
4. MONO or *monophonic*. One note for each channel.

Setting out the assignments as we have done above is incomplete and misleading. MIDI users will know that the instructions have to be in pairs (*MODES*) such as 'OMNI ON/POLY' or 'OMNI OFF/MONO', so that the instruction covers both the response to channels and whether chords or single notes are to be played.

There are plenty of books dealing with MIDI and the reader who needs to find out more should have no difficulty in doing so. We can end here by saying that quite amazing musical effects can be produced by one person provided with

1. enough MIDI-linked devices (musical instruments such as synthesizers) or even computers,
2. talent!

ISDN (integrated services digital network)

This can be thought of as an extension to the public telephone system (BT in the UK) which is used by broadcasters for purposes such as speech contributions from remote studios. The bit rate in the UK is 64 kBits/s (56 kBits/s in the US) and two fairly high quality circuits plus a 'control' circuit can operate in each direction. The contributor's microphone is plugged into a special unit which produces the digital signal and this can travel along standard telephone cables to the nearest exchange for a distance of several kilometres before degradation becomes too severe. (Don't forget that with a digital system there can be marked deterioration of the pulses before they become unidentifiable.)

DAB (digital audio broadcasting)

This is a method of transmitting high quality sound broadcasts without the problems encountered in f.m. broadcasting, particularly with things like car radios. Anyone who has listened to a car radio tuned to an f.m. station will know that there is often distortion of one kind or another caused by buildings causing reflections and so on. DAB overcomes this by a complex technique: a single channel may use more than 1500 carrier frequencies, each one carrying a very low data rate. This means that for reflections to have an effect the reflecting object must be a long way away – as much as 70 or so kilometres, and at that distance the reflected signals will be so weak at the receiver as to have no significant effect.

DAB is scheduled to start in the UK in 1995.

Further reading

The list below is by no means a complete one. It contains a selection of books which you may find helpful, which is not to say that other books not mentioned may not also be worth reading.

Alkin, E. G. M. *Sound with Vision*, Butterworths, 1973

Alkin, E. G. M. *Sound Techniques for Video and TV*, 2nd edn, Focal Press (Media Manual), 1989; originally published as *TV Sound Operations*

Alkin, E. G. M. *Sound Recording and Reproduction*, Focal Press (Media Manual), 1981

Baert, L. *et al. Digital Audio and Compact Disc Technology*, Heinemann-Newnes, 1988

Bermingham, A. *et al. The Video Studio*, Focal Press (Media Manual), 1990; originally published as *The Small Television Studio*, 1975

Borwick, J. (Ed.) *The Loudspeaker and Headphone Handbook*, Butterworths, 1988

Borwick, J. *Microphones: technology and technique*, Focal Press, 1990

Borwick, J. (Ed.) *Sound Recording Practice*, Oxford University Press, 1976

Gayford, M. L. *Electroacoustics: microphones, earphones and loudspeakers*, Newnes-Butterworths, 1970

Gilford, C. *Acoustics for Radio and Television Studios*, Peter Peregrinus, for the IEE, 1972

Nisbett, A. *The Use of Microphones*, 3rd edn, Focal Press (Media Manual), 1989

Nisbett, A. *The Technique of the Sound Studio*, 4th edn, Focal Press, 1979

Robertson, A. E. *Microphones*, Iliffe, 1951

Rumsey, F. *Stereo Sound for Television*, Focal Press, 1989

Rumsey, F. *Tapeless Sound Recording*, Focal Press, 1990

Rumsey, F. *MIDI: Systems and Control*, Focal Press, 1990

Smith, B. J. *Acoustics*, Longmans, 1970

Taylor, C. A. *The Physics of Musical Sounds*, English Universities Press, 1965

Watkinson, J. *The Art of Digital Audio*, Focal Press, 1988

A very useful book of audio data is *The Audio System Designer*, produced by Klark Teknik plc, Kidderminster, UK

Index

For Product Safety Concerns and Information please contact our EU
representative GPSR@taylorandfrancis.com
Taylor & Francis Verlag GmbH, Kaufingerstraße 24, 80331 München, Germany

www.ingramcontent.com/pod-product-compliance
Ingram Content Group UK Ltd.
Pitfield, Milton Keynes, MK11 3LW, UK
UKHW021828240425
457818UK00006B/119